Mistakes In Life:

The Path To Wisdom

Stories Contributed By People From All Over The World

Over 200 Stories For Your Enlightenment And/Or Entertainment

Compiled by My Lan T. Tran

MLTT LLC
2013

Mistakes In Life: The Path To Wisdom
http://www.MistakesInLife.net

Copyright © 2013 by MLTT LLC

MLTT LLC and MLTT LLC logo are trademarks or registered trademarks owned by or licensed to MLTT LLC.
www.mltt.biz

Compiled by My Lan T. Tran, Powered by MLTT LLC.

My Lan T. Tran is the Founder and CEO of MLTT LLC. MLTT LLC's mission is to change the world for the better - one idea at a time.

Printed in the United States of America.

International Standard Book Number (ISBN):
ISBN-13: 978-1492777762
ISBN-10: 1492777765

All rights reserved.
No part of this publication may be visually/vocally/graphically recorded or reproduced in any form or by any means, and distributed without prior written permission from MLTT LLC.

Disclaimer: 1) The information contained in this book is intended to be educational and/or entertaining. The advice given may work for some people, but isn't guaranteed to work for everyone. Everyone's circumstances, situations, environment, and background may be different. Use the advice at your own risk. The compiler, MLTT LLC, and publisher are in no way liable for any misuse of the material. 2) Front cover illustration redesigned from http://www.hdwallpapers3d.com/

For more information about special discounts for bulk purchases, please contact MLTT LLC at
Phone: 1-408-899-9019
Email: support@mistakesinlife.net, mylan@mltt.biz
Note: Due to spamming issue, email and phone number may change. For most up to date contact information, please visit the Contact Us page found on www.MistakesInLife.net

DEDICATION

This book is dedicated to...
- ♥ all of you

And especially to...
- ♥ the children growing up who lack family love, care, and guidance
- ♥ anyone who has ever cried themselves to sleep wishing they had another chance, wishing they could turn back time
- ♥ anyone living with a broken heart and not feeling loved

I just want you to know, even though we may not be related and I may not know who you are or get to have the honor to meet you in this lifetime, I care about you, think about you and want you to be well and happy and living the awesome life you so deserve! You are loved... at least by me!

My Lan T. Tran

ACKNOWLEDGEMENT

The completion of this book couldn't have happened without the help of...

- the contributors from www.MistakesInLife.net

- the contractors who built www.MistakesInLife.net

- many friends and family support, especially Suzane Tran, Ngoc Tran, Chau Tran, Bill Tran, and Robert Paradis.

- (not in a sarcastic way, but bluntly and gracefully put) the teachers in my life who gave me unforgettable life lessons which motivated me to do something to help others

My heart felt thanks to all of you!

My Lan T. Tran

ABOUT THIS BOOK

The stories published in this book are the best chosen from www.MistakesInLife.net up to ID # 599. Many stories from contributors came with grammar and/or typo errors, therefore stories in this book have been slightly edited by volunteers who are not perfect with English either. For the most accurate and original version, please go straight to www.MistakesInLife.net and search for the ID number provided with each of the story in this book.

If you are an individual who has (near) perfect English writing skills and would like to volunteer to help on the next book, please contact My Lan Tran at support@mistakesinlife.net. If you would like to contribute stories to possibly be published in the next book, please email your story (with Title and Category name) to support@mistakesinlife.net or create an account on www.MistakesInLife.net and submit your stories there.

More stories are being submitted on the website almost every day. For newest stories please go straight to www.MistakesInLife.net

PREFACE

This book is put together with good intentions. Life is too short to walk the same path and hit the same pot holes that others had hit many times before. If life is a series of learning processes and mistakes are unavoidable, then perhaps it is probably better that the time, energy, and money are spent on learning from new, interesting and smarter mistakes.

Mistakes, though some people prefer calling them "life lessons", are a part of life. We all make mistakes, big or small. By reading this book, you might find that...

- some mistakes are actually good to make
- some mistakes are hilarious
- people from other corners of the world have similar struggles and mistakes to yours
- mistakes keep happening unless a person breaks the habit or learns the lesson
- good advice are provided
- some advice may not be that great and if you want to, you can go to the website (www.mistakesinlfe.net) and help the contributor understand a better lesson from their mistake(s)
- some mistakes other people make are the same or similar to those that your friends or family members are making and you can use the advice in these stories to warn them
- some mistakes are so silly that you never thought anyone could make them and yet someone somewhere in the world did. It might remind yourself of some of the silly mistakes you made that were too embarrassing to share with friends. It might even make you feel more connected to the world because you realize we're just human beings and imperfect after all.
- some mistakes have a small price to pay while others have a more traumatic and long lasting effect on a person
- loved ones sometimes also have to pay the price for the person who made the mistakes
- some mistakes can bring people closer together

- and much more…. It is an interesting experience to learn how people come to make these mistakes, how their lives were affected, and what they did to change things around or move forward.

This book is not life's instructions on what one should absolutely do or live by. However, it is a book about many things one should NOT do with suggested advice found in the stories that one might apply to one's own life in the same or similar situations.

Not everyone gets to be born in a loving and caring family with endless learning opportunities that can help prepare them for the real world and make living more enjoyable. Perhaps, wisdom found in stories from this book can help fill that gap and help people live more fulfilling lives.

My Lan T. Tran

Contents

- DEDICATION iii
- ACKNOWLEDGEMENT iv
- ABOUT THIS BOOK v
- PREFACE vi
- I'm An Insensitive Husband, I'm Sorry… 19
- Size Doesn't Matter 20
- Resting On Laurels Too Soon 21
- Never Envy Someone For It Is Unbecoming Of You 22
- Admit Shortcomings 24
- Gluttonous 25
- Stay Away From Sharp Items If You Are Clumsy 26
- The One That Got Away 26
- My Mom The Greatest 28
- Raising False Alarm 28
- A Gluttonous Quandary 29
- Don't Sleep In The Bus, Episode 1 29
- Judging The Book By Its Cover 30
- Getting What He Wanted 31
- Everything In Moderation 32
- The Mute Button Is Free 33
- Egg Obsession 33
- Work Versus Personal Life Tip #2 34
- Beware Of The Toxic Sociopath In Sheep's Skin 35
- The Power Of Knowledge 36
- Last Minute Fail 37
- Only Lend Things That You Can Live Without 37
- The Protocol 38

Mistakes In Life: The Path To Wisdom

Choosing My Major Degree 39
Support 39
Buying Online 40
Health Is Wealth 41
Taking My Revenge Without Impunity 41
Gambling 43
Say What You Mean 43
The Wireless Button 44
Know Thyself 45
Sleeping In Class 45
Playing God 46
Taking Care Of My Baby 47
I Deserved That Punishment 47
Say I Love You, If You Have The Chance To 48
Addiction 48
I Didn't Know What To Do 49
Fishy Go Bye Bye 49
No To Impulsive Shopping 50
Never Make A Promise You Can't Keep 51
My Neighbor Doesn't Care 51
Following Your Dreams 52
Staying Back 53
It's That Smoke 53
Be Careful When It's Wet 54
Lessons From The Curse Of Diminutive Knowledge 55
Suffering 55
People Aren't Always What They Seem 56
Be Sensitive To Your Employees - Part 1 56

Embarrassing Experience 58

Purple Grape 58

Not Mail 59

Always Check Twice 59

Losing Time 60

Resisting The Urge To Use My Cell Phone In A Foreign Country 61

My Embarrassing Moment 61

Decide Yourself 62

I Should Have Grabbed It 62

Snaring A Guy 63

Take Time 63

Don't Gossip 64

Job Scam 64

Punch Buggy 65

Oy, Why Does This Lotion Burn 65

Don't Hold Them Down 66

One More Chance 66

Value Of A Mother 67

Humility At Work 68

How My Baby Got Diaper Rashes 68

Never Break Hearts 69

Keeping Time 70

Know Your Own Limits 71

Review Your Answers Before Submitting Them 71

I Wish I Had Talked To Him 72

Watch Out For That Bad Air! 72

Getting Over A Friendship Break Up 73

Mistakes In Life: The Path To Wisdom

Believe In Yourself 74
Lost Love 75
Mind Your Belongings 76
What You Wear Is Not What You Get 77
Be Careful When Entering Someone's Premises 78
Stealing 78
Of Poop And Philosophy 79
Mind Your Own Business 80
Breaking Up Is Hard To Do 80
Mobile Phone 82
Trust Your Instincts 83
I Was Drunk 83
The House Of Our Dreams 84
Missing Chocolate 85
Prevention Is Always Better Than Cure 85
Just Don't Answer 86
If I Was A Little More Careful! 87
Nice To Have Several Bags, But 88
Life Is Short 88
Stick To Your Plan 89
Cheating 89
Bleach Stains 90
To Love And Be Loved 91
Don't Push It When You Are Sick 91
Vous Parlez Le 'Bleep'? 92
Don't Pick! 93
Double-check Hundred Times 94
Saving For The Rainy Days 94

Over Night Traveling 96
Do A Budget Before Making Life-changing Purchases...............96
Turn Off The Microphone 97
Back In My High School 97
Jumping The Queue 98
Patience Is A Virtue..98
He Has Given Me New Hope 99
Please Try To Control Your Anger 100
It's Not Worth The Humiliation 101
Dependence On Alcohol 102
6th Sense..102
Karma's A Fish 103
Save For The Storm 104
Preparing Your Stuff For Work The Night Before 104
It Takes A Little Courage 105
Lying To Miss School 106
Cheapskate Alert! 106
Choose Your Battles 107
Buying Low-priced Hardware 108
Something Smells A Little Fishy 108
Burn-out..109
Blind Date 110
Love Your Life 110
Look Before You Leap 111
Never Count Your Chickens Before They're Hatched 112
Work Versus Personal Life Tip #3 113
What Are The Feelings Of Loneliness 114
Big Time Spenders 115

Mistakes In Life: The Path To Wisdom

Stop Pleasing People - Do What Pleases You!..................116
Speculation Is A Gamble..................116
Report Cards..................117
There Are Times When You Cannot Trust A Doctor..................117
Lesson From Impatience Mind..................119
Check All Of Your Thermostats Before You Leave For Vacation..................119
Blame..................120
Saving The Best For Last..................120
Be Careful About Jokes On Age..................121
Sharp Tongue, Harsh Words..................122
Hate For Mathematics..................123
No Rush..................123
Be Sensitive To Your Employees - Part 2..................124
Don't Waste Your Time..................126
Always Know Where The Route Is..................126
Three's A Crowd..................127
Count The Change Before Leaving..................128
Why Should We Need To Obey Our Parents..................129
Water Is Good For The Body But…..................129
Don't Be A Fool..................130
Think Twice..................131
Life Is Chances..................131
Change Comes From Within..................132
Lesson From Over Optimism..................133
Don't Loan Your 16-year-old The Car..................134
Cheating..................134
My Phone's Battery Died..................135

Walls Have Ears 135
A Beacon Leading The Way For The Right Path 136
Fraud 138
The One That Got Away 2 138
Don't Believe Everything You See On TV 139
Don't Judge A Person 140
Is This Salt In My Coffee? 140
Game Zombie 141
A Lesson On Over-serving 141
Don't Think About Only You, Think About The World Too . 142
Loving Too Much 142
Love Of Parents 143
Disaster Party 144
Blind Date #2 144
Green IS Hot 145
Things I Needed To Say 146
I Like Koo-koo Nuts, Do You? 147
WHY WON'T YOU FLUSH!!!!! 148
Wash Your Hands 149
The Blues Is NOT For Church 149
Tragedy Is The Mother Of Necessity 150
Lost Phone 151
To Go Natural Or Not 152
But It Lives In The Snow 152
Grab The Opportunity 153
Sharpies Are NOT Face Paint 153
Never Follow The Crowd 154
My Second Chance 155

Mistakes In Life: The Path To Wisdom

Insomnia Attack!... 156
Choose Positive People To Influence Yourself 157
Money Is Not Everything 158
Obedience 158
When "Don't Sweat The Small Stuff" Isn't True 159
Lesson From Enviousness 160
Saying No - Making It A Habit 160
Broken Relationship 161
Cracking Elbow 162
Want To Volunteer? Think Again 162
Mistakes From My Immaturity 163
Eating The Deity's Candy 163
Love At 18 164
Don't Sleep In The Bus, Episode 2 165
Don't Just Follow The Heart 165
Low Self Esteem 166
Puppies Are Hard Work 167
A Lesson In Pride 167
Fun And A Broken Bone 168
Safety In The Bathroom 169
Advice From A Teacher 170
Get Together Unveils Secrets 170
Missing 60? 171
Check The Items Against The Receipt 172
Crying Over Spilt Milk 172
No Beans On Your First Date 174
Telling Lies 174
Sleep Is Not Optional 175

Make Sure That Alarm Will Work 175
Preparedness Is Key 176
Fetching Firewood 177
The Orgmate 177
Leaking Faucet And A High Water Bill 178
Depends On Yourself Not Others 179
The One Day Millionaire Habit 179
No Hero 180
Sale? Check The Label! 181
An Ode To My Mother 182
Don't Use Very Strong Shampoo 185
Living A Negative Free Life 185
Save Something For Your Future Generation 186
Wishing I Had A Phone 187
I Gotta Go 188
Enjoy Life, Have A Break 188
Traveling With Mom 189
Wedding 189
Some Rules Are Not Meant To Be Broken 190
Don't Eat The Cookies 190
Definitely Never Going To Act 191
You Fear THAT (tiny) Thing? o.O 192
2nd Chances 192
Get Out Of The Mud 194
Don't Smoke 195
Curiosity Did Not Kill The Cat...It Scared Me Off 195
Don't Be A Thief 197
Do What Your Doctor Says 197

Mistakes In Life: The Path To Wisdom

I Could Have Avoided That..198
I'm Busy, Go Away! 198
IV Insertion 199
Be Faithful 199
Poverty...200
If You Are Not Familiar, Go With The Usual 200
A Few Stolen Moments 201
Stress Ruined My Relationship 202
Car Accident..203
Unsafe Baby Bath 203
Don't Overdress It...204
Nurturing A Child 205
Since When Was Facebook Homework?............................206
I'm Getting Too Old For This 206
Hot Coffee vs. Tongue..207
Drive Carefully..207
Don't Drink And Speak...208
A Mother's Love 209
Saving Money Gone Wrong...209
To Share Or Not To Share 210
Don't Sleep In The Bus, Episode #3....................................211
High-heeled Disaster 212
Procrastinate Not - Things Will Surely Catch Up..............213
Exceptional Anger...214
CLOSING NOTES 215

My Lan T. Tran

I'M AN INSENSITIVE HUSBAND, I'M SORRY...

ID: 156

So I have an experience that I'd like to share with everyone. Being a husband, I just realized this and I think this can help any man who has a woman or a wife in his life.

I happened to be thinking of my actions lately and looked at my relationship with my wife. I think I am really neglecting her. During my "rest day" from work, which is every Sunday, I usually just stay home with my wife and our daughter. I don't go out with friends anymore because I usually do that every Saturday night. I just hang around the house. Watch TV or have few bottles of beer while singing with the karaoke. My wife doesn't mind this actually....or so I thought. But while talking to her several days ago, I've found out that she's feeling abandoned and lonely, that she doesn't have time for herself anymore. She doesn't even get rest days from doing all the household chores at home. She said that while I enjoy myself in front of the TV, she's the only one who's taking care of our baby, making the baby's bottle, bathing the baby, preparing our meal, doing the laundry, cleaning the house and everything else.

She also emphasized that I don't even offer to do the dishes which only takes a little effort and time. She had asked for my help several times, but I seemed to be preoccupied and always neglecting her. She felt like she has been taken for granted. I barely even offer her to go out for a family dinner date or go shopping together anymore. She doesn't feel like she's my wife, but more like a household help lady.

At first I was defensive of all these statements, but later I realized that I was indeed wrong. I feel like I'm a terrible person for doing this to my own wife and this is why our relationship has become boring and routine. We lack diversion. I'm an insensitive husband because I do not see the needs of my wife and appreciate her for all the things she's doing.

I'm now ready to amend my ways and show my wife that I appreciate and truly love her....not only by words but with actions. I will help with the household chores and do my share of taking care of our baby. I am willing

Mistakes In Life: The Path To Wisdom

to do everything possible to improve our marital relationship and make it exciting and inspiring again.

I hope that every husband out there who's doing the same thing with their wife will join me and change our ways. Let's offer to do the dishes and take out the trash as often as we can. Let's treat our wives to a nice dinner or give her something not necessarily expensive. I'm sure she'll appreciate it in one way or another.

SIZE DOESN'T MATTER

ID: 86

My most recent life lesson was taught to me by my puppy. She is a Chihuahua and is very small to say the least. In fact at her last vet visit she was right at 2 pounds and could still fit in the pocket of my hoodie. Before I explain the lesson, let me explain a little bit about myself. I am a teacher and though I can take on a classroom full of not too thrilled middle schoolers, I seldom stand up for myself against those that are higher up, have more experience, or are in any way bigger than myself. I am the employee that receives all the work and none of the credit because I am content to let someone else be in the limelight. In fact feeling sorry for the weakest of the bunch is how I ended up with my little pup. My little girl was the smallest out of eight puppies in the litter. Even full grown she will top out at three pounds. Little One is the one who taught me a lesson in standing up for myself.

A few months ago she had to be rushed to the vet after, we found out later, having eaten half a cough drop that made her very ill. We were sitting in the waiting room all alone when a woman walked in with a mama Rottweiler that was almost my size and could have made a chew toy out of Little One. This Rottweiler looked at Little One with hunger in her eyes and as she sniffed the carrier it looked to me like her mouth watered. Little One was barking incessantly, as Chihuahua's do. I finally gave in and pulled her from the carrier to sit on my lap. The Rottweiler, who the owner said was nice, walked over to sniff Little One. Little One promptly hit the Rottweiler on the nose with a paw and snapped at the monstrous beast. The

Rottweiler quickly yipped and went back to sit with her owner. I couldn't help but smile as I realized that this little nothing of a dog had more courage than I have ever had in my life. Little One didn't know she was smaller, she did not know that she could be a snack for that beast, she instead stood her ground and the larger animal backed off. While I know this isn't true for every situation, I did learn to stand up and be at least as brave as my Little One.

RESTING ON LAURELS TOO SOON
ID: 336

I graduated from one of my country's top universities. Because of this, I have always been proud of myself and my achievements. Although I never bragged much around people, it was a different story in my head. I'd sometimes have these self-righteous thoughts; Every now and then, I'd compare myself with people who make silly mistakes.

Last year, I got employed by a large company that specializes in construction to be part of their management program. During the first month, I gauged the capabilities of my peers and thought I must easily be among the top in the group. I was more mature, from the best school, and as far as I knew, the only one with experience that was the most related to our job. Because of these, I didn't care how many tests and presentations they had us undergo. I never took any of these seriously, not even the grades that my supervisors gave me. I thought I could easily make up for this with on-site performance and the ability to establish rapport.

A year passed and a report was prepared to present our individual progress. I light-heartedly asked our manager how "bottom" I was in the rankings. I expected him to reassure me about how well I was doing. He didn't. So I asked him again how well I did. He said if grades were the only basis, I was last. Then he began explaining how all the tests, presentations, and other requirements affected my rating. While I may have performed well on-site, the scores and my attendance said otherwise. I was devastated. The ratings were supposed to be the only leverage I had for

Mistakes In Life: The Path To Wisdom

asking for better compensation. Now I can't even bring the subject of appraisal up to them.

Pride only gets us so far. We may be the smartest person in the world, but in the end, diligence and a healthy working attitude is what guarantees that we get to the finish line.

NEVER ENVY SOMEONE FOR IT IS UNBECOMING OF YOU

ID: 563

I envied her right from the start without understanding what she was and why she was being favored more than me. I was selfish and wanted more from my parents as I hungered for everything they could offer me. I was 10. I was still a kid, not a grown up. I needed guidance. I needed love. I needed care. I looked at them as they happily played together inside their bedroom. They all laughed as they doted at her. She looked adorable as she looked at them with her big innocent eyes. While I was outside the door, I paused there for a long time, careful not to make a sound as I did not want to disturb them. In my eyes, the view was perfect. Every last piece of the puzzle fit. Suddenly, realization hit me. Where was I supposed to be?

I grew up without my parents as they have worked hard overseas ever since I could remember. It was tough for me to live with them after not being with them for so long. I felt alienated and uncomfortable. What irked me the most at that time was the fact that my Mom had just given birth to my younger sister. She was born on the same day that my father was born. Her nickname was close to my Dad's nickname and they said that if she were only a boy, they would call him their junior. Due to the age that my Mom got pregnant, it was difficult for her give birth to her. When the doctors were delayed in performing a caesarian on her, my Mom and my younger sister almost lost both of their lives. They were both dehydrated. Thankfully, they both lived to tell the tale. Unfortunately, it left my sister in the incubator for two weeks and then after that, the doctor said that due to the lack of oxygen and dehydration inside my mother's womb, that somehow affected her motor skills and that her mind development might not be normal. My parents were strong. They were not prepared for what had happened but they loved my sister fiercely and knew they had to do everything they could to make her feel loved.

I was in another country, my homeland, when my younger sister was born. I knew that my Mom was pregnant. I just had no clue when she would be giving birth. For the longest time, I was the little one that they adored but I knew things would change after that. When I was brought to Oman to live with them, I yearned for them. I was needy and unfortunately, due to the birth of my younger sister, their attention became more focused on her than on me. I was stubborn and selfish as I craved everything that they could give me. They had been so far away for so long. I wished that things were just like the way they used to be. I didn't know the story behind my younger sister's struggle. To me, she was stealing my parents away from me and I hated it. Despite what I have felt, I still cared for her. I didn't spoil her though. That part I would have to leave to my parents. I loved her but never really told her about it. My parents knew about how I felt and they decided that I had the right to know what had happened to her and why they took care of her more than they do for me. That night, they explained everything to me. In my young mind, I understood that I was wrong. I felt awful to think bad things about her. Now, I know I should have been the adult in the situation. I was the older sister after all. I regretted being what I was in the past and vowed to become a better older sister to her than I was before.

Time flew by fast and as I got older, she grew too. My younger sister suffers from Mild Cerebral Palsy. Although she does not drool and shake uncontrollably like the others who have a more severe case than her, the disease somehow affected her development and her motor skills. She does not walk. She is in a wheelchair. She is turning 17 this year and because she really wants to walk on her eighteenth birthday, she is currently undergoing a lot of therapy. Despite all the bruises, she continues to try hard to become normal. She is graduating from elementary school soon and she is excited to go to high school. We are all supportive of her. She can stand now but she still needs to improve her balance to be able to continuously walk on her own. She is a survivor and a fighter. I now admire her for everything that she has been through and I am proud to say that she is my younger sister.

Mistakes In Life: The Path To Wisdom

There have been times when she has cried as she felt self pity upon herself. She has often uttered sentences and questions asking why she had to be different from others and that she did not want to be like that forever. She wanted to walk, to run and to dance. She wanted to do normal things that most people probably take for granted. She wishes to feel her feet and be able to stand on her own. She wants to jump, to swim and just be free. She did not want to wear diapers anymore as she was a grown lady. She needed to be more independent. She wanted to have a life of her own. How? She did not know. The thought both scares her and makes her feel upset. My parents constantly tell me to never make her feel upset. If possible, she should never feel such sadness. Call it false hope if you will but to us it is our form of encouragement. We want her to walk and to strive hard to become normal. I just regret that I never did in the past. Now that I know everything about this, I realize how tough it must have been for my parents to raise her and to make sure that she was happy. The unwanted and disgusted stares from passersby and other people only made the ordeal greater. Fortunately for us, she grew up to be a happy child.

Lesson learned. Do not be quick to judge others as you do not know what their real story is. Do not envy, instead understand. Do not hate, instead love. To those who aren't normal, do not treat them differently for they are living things, they are people too. They have feelings and you certainly do not want that on your conscience. I love my sister no matter how special she is. I wish her well and I have grown to accept the fact that I may have felt detached in the past but I am a part of our family and we are one unit so we should function as such. Life is always filled with realizations. You just need to pause a moment and try to clear your head; welcome thoughts. Only then will you realize that there is more to life than what you thought there should be.

ADMIT SHORTCOMINGS

ID: 511

I was in my internship in the laboratory. It's a pretty crucial year since I'm slowly getting closer and closer to graduation. I wanted to do my best and overcome everything. Again, a lot of the times during my training, my pride had gotten in the way of things going smoothly. The laboratory is found inside a hospital which is supposedly a bit high class compared to other hospitals, but still we lacked finances to cover expenses of an adequate number of tests. There are some wherein you just put some drops of blood and reagents, it's pretty straight forward right? That's what I thought too. That's why I told my staff in charge of my section that I knew how to perform the test, when I had never really tried it myself. I thought that it was easy and didn't take much skill. I was completely wrong. I ended up wasting some test kits and got a scolding from my staff in charge. It's wrong to let your pride get in the way and compensate for a lack of experience. I couldn't do anything with the funding of the hospital for the laboratory section, but my part as a member of the laboratory is to perform the tests correctly within an amount of time. Sometimes, you have to admit you are not capable of something instead of trying to impress people by lying. I reflected a lot on my actions after that incident, and I never made the same mistake again. I learned how to say, "I don't know." I realized that's the first step to learning, so that next time you can say truthfully, "Yes, I do know."

GLUTTONOUS

ID: 28

When I was younger, I loved eating mangos. When they were in season, I would save every coin to ensure that on market day I would have some money to buy myself several mangos to enjoy with other kids on our way from school. Even when I didn't have any money, I would still pass by the market and look in the bins to see if there were any good ones thrown out by mistake or those that weren't as rotten. One day I ate a rotten one and I got a very bad stomach ache that I had to go to the hospital because of bad diarrhea. I was given so many painful injections that I swore to never repeat the same mistake. I learned that greed is not any good and that it can cause me pain and harm.

STAY AWAY FROM SHARP ITEMS IF YOU ARE CLUMSY

ID: 308

Never shave when you are tired and low on blood sugar. I tried a single blade disposable razor several years ago and they don't quite shave like my regular triple blade. It started with a single slice across my knee but I kept trying to shave because it wasn't so bad. After I moved on to my other leg and started shaving near my ankle, I slipped and cut off all of the skin around my ankle bone. It was bleeding very heavily. I have never gone back to single blade razor again and I make sure that I am fully awake and ready to shave before I touch my body with a sharp object.

THE ONE THAT GOT AWAY

ID: 108

When I was 18, I had my first boyfriend. He was a few years older, very cute and attractive and good to me. He was very respectful and helpful to my parents/family as well. I was very fortunate to have him, unfortunately I didn't realize that at the time and took him for granted. I remember every time he saw me he would have a small present for me. He was not rich, but he did try to give me the best of everything. He always put me first and apologized even when I was wrong. Throughout the whole time we were together he treated me like a goddess, but me being young and not knowing better, I didn't appreciate him. Whatever I wanted, I got it and I was quite demanding back then. It was always either my way or the highway. He gave me things I didn't even think I would want/need. He gave me lots of attention and cared for me and loved me. The best part was he knew I didn't feel the same way towards him, but he still loved me, was patient with me, and stood by me anyways. I remember him calling me his wife shortly into the relationship and I hated that, thinking that he was moving too quickly. In the end I broke it off with him and that broke his heart terribly and that was a big mistake.

Call it bad luck or karma or coincidence or whatever, but a decade later and after several relationships and a couple badly broken hearts I realized how lucky I was when I was with my first boyfriend. Every time my boyfriends mistreat me, I always remember how my first boyfriend always loved me and never dared to do anything to make me sad. He always tried to make me happy and thoughts of that hurt quite a bit, and it made me miss him a lot and as time went on I realized I was wrong and I loved him, but it's too late now. The last I heard of him is that he's married now and we (my friends and I) all lost contact with him and have forgotten his last name. I really wish I had met him after having gone through all the other @ssholes in my life, so I could understand and appreciate him and we would have made it to the altar.

I hope our path would cross again someday so I can say "I'm so sorry" to him and thank him for having loved me so much even when I didn't deserve it. I doubt that I'll meet anyone else who can or will love me as much as he did. His love for me was sincere and real without questioning or demanding of anything in return. I learned that when it comes to feelings, it doesn't matter if it comes fast or slow as long as it's real. I remember he wept a little bit over the phone when I wouldn't see him on our first month anniversary. At the time, I hated that – a boy who cried. Now I wish I would meet someone who would love me so much to shed a tear for me, who would miss me so much that they can't sleep at night.

The lesson here is never take anyone for granted, especially the people who love you and care for you. What goes around comes around. If you do, someday you'll fall deeply in love with someone else who will take you for granted just like that or even worse. It happened to me. I hope you learn from me and be kind to people and open your heart to those who love you. It may take a decade to learn to love them back, but it'll happen and you'll be more glad to give your heart to those who are proven worthy... than the ones who you went through hell for hoping they would return your love.

Mistakes In Life: The Path To Wisdom

MY MOM THE GREATEST

ID: 481

When I was child, I was very much offended by my parents. They used to control me through a very tight daily schedule where I could hardly get any time with my friends and/or play. I used to be a very impatient and wicked boy at that age. Because the barriers put by my mom at that age, I used to hate my mom. This hate for my mom began to build up so much that I began to pray for the death of my mom so that I could be free from the cage. But now, coming to maturity I can see the success in my life. I can foresee how my mom set me on the right path all through my life. How my mom helped me when I had fevers and diseases, how my mom passed all those sleepless nights before my exams, how she became worried for the whole week when I was out on my trips and travels. How in every course of my life she gave me the option to be a successful man. Never ignore your mother. Listening to a mother is how a great man is created.

RAISING FALSE ALARM

ID: 51

One time my parents went away for a night and I was left to watch the other siblings because I was the first born. In the middle of the night, we heard a bang in the house and I thought that we were being attacked by thugs. I screamed to alert the neighbors who came running to our rescue because they had been informed to keep checking on us. They asked what had happened and they checked the entire house but didn't find anything. After a short while we heard the sound again only to find that it was the cat that had dropped a pan in the kitchen. The neighbors were furious because of the false alarm and they warned us not to do it again. I learned that I should have tried to find out the source of the noise before disturbing others because if and when I am genuinely in trouble they may not come to my rescue if I continue raising false alarms.

My Lan T. Tran

A GLUTTONOUS QUANDARY

ID: 393

My mom is a really good cook. But from all the recipes that she has cooked, I've had a memorable experience with one, the bean pork stew. On that day, there was enough to feed almost three households. This only meant one thing: more for me!! By the time Ma finished cooking, I was onto that pot like an eager beaver. Ma said that I was eating far too much for my own good and asked me to bring some to my grandma and aunt's house. I did, but filled the container that was their share at only half its capacity. Reasoning to myself that grandma doesn't really enjoy this stuff and plus auntie has always been stingy with her cooking.

It was already past 8 in the evening, but I was still digging into that bean stew religiously. At around 9:30, filled to the brim, I crept to bed. Flitting in and out of my dreams, I woke up sweating. In a panic, I rushed to the kitchen sink. I stood there for a couple of seconds, confused with what I was experiencing. Then it came, from up my throat and out into the sink. Beans, not even properly digested. It went on for a few minutes. My mom heard the racket and came to check, finding me bent over the sink. After I was done, I looked at her incredulous face. "See? This is exactly what happens if you eat beans at so late an hour! And you've been eating nothing but that the entire day!" I smiled weakly at her as I stumbled back to my room.

In an afterthought I realized if I hadn't woken to throw up, I could've died in my sleep! Lesson: Never eat like there's no tomorrow. Gluttony has its awful and disgusting repercussions.

DON'T SLEEP IN THE BUS, EPISODE 1

ID: 159

It was the 15th of March in 2003 (Saturday), one of the most memorable days in my life: I got my first salary, in cold cash. I was working as a call center agent, and so the end of my week would basically be Saturday morning. As all graveyard shifters feel at this time of day and week, I felt

Mistakes In Life: The Path To Wisdom

almost dead and airheaded due to the lack of sleep. I then fell asleep on the bus going home. In fact, in such a deep sleep (as if I was in my bed) that I couldn't even remember how I got to the bus in the first place.

I couldn't remember a thing from the time I paid my fare until I got off. I was so looking forward to be reunited with my bed, when – as I opened my bag to savor even just a moment of my first pay, I didn't find the envelope in there – all I wanted was to chase the bus and go get my money! (Not even thinking about the possibilities on where I actually lost it!)

It's magical what adrenaline can do – I instantly remembered – vividly – what happened in the bus. Before the bus was just about to leave, a heavily bearded man hopped in and sat right beside me. He even said sorry when he saw that I woke up when he sat down. I remember that I felt someone trying to pull my bag, but I don't know if I resisted or if I acted upon it. It seems someone actually put my bag on my lap. I had a brief moment thinking that, maybe the bag fell, but I didn't care much because someone helped get it back for me.

There's only one possibility... someone got into my bag and took my money – my seatmate at the bus! At that moment, I couldn't feel any worse. It was indeed life-changing, definitely an eye-opener for me. From that moment on, I have never slept in the bus unless I am with someone I know, and I always keep my bag tightly secured with me.

JUDGING THE BOOK BY ITS COVER

ID: 595

For a long time I took a glance at people and judged them without question. Mostly it was stereotypes that I had accumulated from television or magazines. If one had such and such hair do, it meant this about them and so on.

It is hard not to judge someone in a few seconds of meeting them but again, I only came to realize my mistake when I was also judged harshly in my face. I was in a bus heading home and the passenger next to me had these huge locks of hair and looked unshaven, unkempt and I definitely went straight to defense mode and I naturally grabbed my purse so that he could not steal from me. My reaction got his attention and he only let out a sigh.

The man must have been really irritated by this move and he turned around and said I must have no decency and respect for elders. I inquired why, as I knew this was totally out of line. He broke it down from the clothes I had and also how my hair was done. It was then that I realized that I had done exactly the same to him. He told me the kind of job he had and it was unexpected that he was working for a well known corporate firm that I actually had an interest in applying for a job. That conversation still rings in my head and I still look back and wonder what if he had never opened his mouth to talk to me and shine the light on the mistakes I was doing. He actually gave me good tips on how to present myself for a job interview at the firm and although I did not get the job, I did learn not to judge the book by its cover.

GETTING WHAT HE WANTED

ID: 69

He was a guy I was set up with on a blind date. I was only eighteen at the time, but I knew there was something about him that wasn't good. We didn't even last long, but it was long enough for him to hurt me a few times. I didn't really have feelings for him, and I didn't think it was going to last long between us. We went out one night on a double date, but I felt a connection to my friend's date. I thought he was cute and felt like I had seen him somewhere. We clicked and the guy I was with got jealous. I didn't know it then, but later that night I discovered he was jealous at the way I was friendly towards this other guy so he decided he was going to have his way with me and he hurt me. I'd like to say I didn't talk to him after that, but it took me one more time of him hurting me to just leave. I think that when I left him, I started going out with the other guy, but the other guy that hurt me still called me nonstop. He was like a leech I couldn't get rid of. He called me and wanted to come over. I really didn't want him to come over because he tended to manipulate me into letting

Mistakes In Life: The Path To Wisdom

him come over. He pressured me into to losing my virginity to him. I didn't want to do it with him because I didn't love him and he had hurt me. He ended up getting what he wanted because he date raped me. It's hard to prove a thing like that. The guy I liked felt jealous about the other guy. I told him that he raped me and that it didn't mean anything because I was pressured. He kept calling me so I had to keep call blocking him numerous times. He just wouldn't leave me alone and one time he said he was going to hurt me and my boyfriend. A while later he called me. I was single at the time and he forced me to go to a party with him. There, I had three drinks. That's not enough for me to get drunk, but I was tired and feeling a little buzzed. After the party he drove me home. We didn't go all the way home however, because he parked somewhere. I told him I wasn't in the mood and that I really didn't want to do it with him. I eventually gave in, but being in the car with him was the last thing I wanted. He didn't care for me or love me. I was screaming in pain the whole time and telling him I wanted to stop. After all these years, I still cry about it. Lesson learned: Don't ever allow yourself to be hurt more than once. It's never okay.

EVERYTHING IN MODERATION

ID: 367

As I've already said in an earlier article, my parents were very very strict. When I started college, I was really enjoying my freedom and being able to do things without their permission. When I met some of my friends I started going to parties with them, and staying up later and later. During my first semester this didn't affect me because I was doing it in moderation, on the weekends and on days that I didn't have classes. The next couple of semesters went downhill fast though. I started staying up late, skipping classes and not doing my homework. The second semester I was put on academic probation, which means that if you don't get your grades in better shape you could lose your financial aid. The third semester was my last shot, but I still didn't listen and blew it. I lost my financial aid, and ended up taking a year off before I realized that I had to get myself in gear and go back to school. I went back, brought my grades up and am continuing my education today. I learned that everything in moderation is ok, but when you let partying with friends take over you lose big time.

My Lan T. Tran

THE MUTE BUTTON IS FREE

ID: 174

Working as a technical lead in a customer service department entails frequent conference calls with customers. The calls become more exciting when the more difficult customers and those that really stand out are involved. They've earned a reputation within our department and have respective nicknames and/or signature quotes that identify them.

In one of those calls, and with a controversial topic at hand, my entire team decided to listen in. This was a different scenario for me. I usually wore a headset but this time the phone had to be on speaker mode. Because of this, I forgot to press the MUTE button and as soon as the team heard from our favorite customer, everybody started making side comments. Oh-mi-gosh. I realized I wasn't muted because our favorite customer suddenly just stopped talking.

My face turned red, and everyone else beside me stopped talking too! A few seconds after, the leader in the call asked what was going on, and then I immediately and confidently said "hmmm... must be some interference." I was so relieved nobody pursued the case.

From that moment on, I either always turn the MUTE button on or close my office and restrict my team from getting on those calls. I occasionally ask some of them to join in but with a strict policy to avoid side comments.

EGG OBSESSION

ID: 549

I am so very fond of eggs. Actually I prefer eggs more than any other food. Eggs are really very delicious to me. When I was a twelve year old boy, I learned to make omelets. From that day, I would make omelets and eat them. But my mother was not so happy about this, she told me, "Son, eating too many eggs is bad. If you like it so much then eat, but when the weather is hot, don't eat a lot of eggs". But eggs were so important for me, so I didn't listen to her. One evening during summer, no one was at home.

Mistakes In Life: The Path To Wisdom

So I got my chance, I made 6 omelets and started to eat. After eating five eggs one by one, my body temperature rose up. I was feeling a pain in my stomach. Soon I got more weak, I could not move. After two or three hours, my mother came home and took me to the hospital. I had to take three injections to reduce the pain. When the doctor was injecting me, I prayed to God and said, "I will never eat so many eggs, please keep me alive."

WORK VERSUS PERSONAL LIFE TIP #2

ID: 194

Family First.

Have you ever been in a situation when you were having so much fun and success with "the career," that you tend to get stuck between choosing a family event and work? A very good example for me is the time when, four months after I got married, I was offered a really high-paying job (five times my current salary) and a very rewarding one in terms of almost every aspect you could think of. The only catch was that I had to travel around the world, conducting training classes or consulting sessions. Believing that my husband was perfectly okay with this setup, I accepted this new job. I must admit that even if I was not with my husband – I enjoyed the traveling privileges, the $80 per diem, going to many places, shopping and meeting a lot of people. I just deeply, truly loved my job. This went on for around two years, and time passed by quickly for me because my trips were back-to-back. On my third year, that's when my husband started asking me if I missed him while I was away, until it led to the baby-thing, to growing old together, to taking advantage of the times when we are together... because life is so short. I must admit that the signs/questions were there for so long, but I either ignored them or I just thought he was just being sentimental/dramatic. While this was all happening to my marriage, my parents' lives also started getting messy. My dad started having affairs (note the "s") and I got really mad at him (until now), but hearing him say that my mom seemed to love her job more than the family struck me hard. An instant replay of my husband's dramatic moments started flashing through my mind. At this very moment I felt fear, that this could be happening to me too. I suddenly remembered, that before I got married, I actually told myself all the time, that once I get married, the focus of my time will be my husband and my new family. I also remember telling my husband that I didn't need to achieve more than what I had in terms of my career, because I was happy where I was – with him.

My husband did not resort to the same measures as my father, but there was indeed a change with how he talked to me, and I did feel that there was a certain "unhappiness" within him. That certain awareness pained me.

Surprisingly, it just hit me hard: I want to grow old with my husband; home is where I should be. Nothing, not even money, can beat the happiness and contentment that married life, and family bring.

A few weeks after this realization, I quit the job. Everybody in the company was surprised. My main reason for leaving – Family First.

BEWARE OF THE TOXIC SOCIOPATH IN SHEEP'S SKIN

ID: 401

I was 19 and met a stranger in college that exuded the aura of a perfect gentleman, but later on as I got to know him better, he showed his true colors being that of an emotionally abusive person. I saw the signs at first but disregarded them and just tried to avoid him when I could. Although he never became a romantic prospect for me, I think it was difficult to be removed from a situation wherein you are already too involved with someone because we both belonged to the same campus organization which I was very passionate about. For reasons I will never know until the day I die, he started spreading all these lies saying that I was very fond of him, was the one chasing him, and that I was the one who had been expecting too much. It made me even more shocked when I was at a mall and I came across him with a girl with whom he tried to do some PDA the moment he saw me approaching.

Mistakes In Life: The Path To Wisdom

The years went on and in the act of "crazy-making", he blamed me and said I deserved all the lies he had created. It was all crazy; he displayed all the characteristics of a sociopath. I researched that kind of behavior and the more I read on the matter, the better I understood where I stood. It helped me become more sure of myself because I discovered sociopaths have very superficial human emotions and they NEVER feel remorse, guilt, or shame. They never respect your space and reputation.

So I think my advice would be to face the reality that there are people who are capable of performing such abuse on you. Never fall into the trap that the sociopath draws you in because they are full of lies. Be wary of the steps they use: first they idolize you, devalue, and then discard you altogether, leaving you in a state of confusion as to what you had done to deserve such treatment. Meanwhile, they leave a trail of devastation in their path and never take responsibility, let alone show an ounce of regret over their actions. Never feel victimized as it is not your fault; just have faith and constantly make the best of every day. Never give the sociopath another thought and when you see them – run!

THE POWER OF KNOWLEDGE

ID: 567

Until fifth grade, I had no interest for learning and I hated studying or anything related to education. My parents tried to give me advice but I really didn't care. I used to play more than any friends of mine. Most of the time I left home and took my backpack and stuff. However, I didn't directly go to school. After I walked halfway to school, I would turn a different way to get to a few friends which had exactly the same behavior as me. I didn't do homework and classwork rather I disturbed the class the whole period. I remember my fifth year science teacher. He seriously tried to know why I hated class and he politely asked me why I disliked education. I had no reason to tell him.

I will never forget the day that was a turning point in my life. That day was the celebration day which was celebrated once a year. In this time, class for the year is ended and the top three students from each class were rewarded with books by the school for their academic achievement. When I saw these students, I felt something new that I had never experienced before. I asked myself one short word, "why?" Why couldn't I be like these students? I cried and cried for a long time I didn't know why but I think I felt useless...

In the next sixth grade, with self-motivation, I studied hard. My parents were amazed and supported me in all of my educational life. Since then, I have scored high points in school and was in the top 5 students listed in all of the grades.

LAST MINUTE FAIL

ID: 4

When I was in sixth grade, there was an assignment that I had decided to put aside until the last minute. By the time the due date came, I hadn't even started it. When the teacher asked where it was, I told her I had lost the file on my computer, and that I would try to find it. I went home, but I didn't try to find or do it. I just decided to take a zero. The next week when my teacher noticed that I still didn't have it, she spoke to my dad and I, telling me that she would give me another chance, and that I should try to re-write it. Unfortunately, my dad made me re-write it, and I still got a failing grade for bringing it in so late. Now I try not to be a last minute worker.

ONLY LEND THINGS THAT YOU CAN LIVE WITHOUT

ID: 90

I'm fond of books. I love almost all sorts of books and stories. And I also have exclusive huge shelves in my room which are only intended for them. Once, a friend visited my house to see my book collection. She scanned

Mistakes In Life: The Path To Wisdom

each of them and was very interested with a particular book I separated on one shelf. It was the "Tropic of Capricorn" by Henry Miller. Personally, I didn't very much like the story, however I did love the book very much because it was a gift by my grandmother on my 18th birthday. My friend insisted to borrow it and assured me she would return it the next day. After so much pleading from her, I unwillingly lent the book. The next morning came and another week had passed but my friend hadn't visited me to return the book. I tried calling her. She said she would return it as soon as she could find time since she was busy with her newly found job. I tried to understand her but the thought that I didn't have one of my most valued possessions kept bothering me. So, a couple of weeks later, I finally went to my friend's apartment to claim my precious book, but to my despair I found out that she already moved to another town for the new job. I had no means of getting to her since she had not left any address or contact information.

To this day, every time I remember that book, I still regret the day I let someone borrowed it. It was one of the intangible things that my late grandma left to me. A simple book, but a symbol of good memory with grandma. Today, I don't let anyone take anything that has a sentimental value to me. Because, if that item is not returned, I'm sure my life would not be the same again without it.

THE PROTOCOL

ID: 449

I worked as a nurse in one of the government hospitals in our community. I was assigned in the surgery department; there were lots of patients admitted when I had this duty. It was our protocol that we must take their blood pressure every four hours. Due to increased number of patients, I thought that it would be best to just take the blood pressure of critically ill patients. I never expected that there was a patient who was in a blood pressure monitoring whom I had forgotten. During my shift, she collapsed and needed an immediate care in order to regain her energy. It was said in her chart that she should take a prescribed medication if she had decreased blood pressure. The patient was brought to the ICU for special interventions. I realized that vital signs were really important for every patient in the hospital. I advise that, you should follow the protocols in your job and thus you will not make your own decisions with regards to the treatment that your clients deserve.

CHOOSING MY MAJOR DEGREE
ID: 510

The day I got myself entered in the university life, I overestimated my performance. I always tried to have knowledge in subjects that I didn't even take. I was deliberate to take any kind of pressure before exams or even final exams. I never declined any work assigned by my faculty as I thought I had superb quality over others. Before selecting my major course my parents advised me to think twice and thrice before selecting this as this can change the course of my life. But I was confident enough to take any major I wished as I was a good student then in my elementary courses. But after doing 2 courses of my major, my grades began to fall and my performance declined in many group activities of my major courses. This was due to poor major selection. Early in my life, I was interested in financial and economics where I chose my major as Human Resource Management. After doing 3 courses and spending $4000 I had to stop doing any further classes and changed my major to finance immediately. I learned a lesson (by spending some valuable time and money) that you never should be too confident in life, because excess self-confidence can put you in danger.

SUPPORT
ID: 31

A few months ago my friend needed me for some 'girl talk'. Obviously I said yes because I wanted to be there for her. She had a crush on a guy that was 3 years older than her, and near the end of the school year he started talking to her. He wanted a nude photo of her, and promised that he would send one back. She asked me if she should send it, but I didn't care whether she did or not, so I said do whatever you feel like doing. She asked me what would I do but I kept insisting it didn't matter what I would do. In the end, she sent it but he never talked to her ever again, and to this day she is emotionally scarred. This was a mistake because I should've told her it was wrong... The lesson learned here is that you should never support your friend in doing wrong things, but to encourage them to do the right thing, the one that won't hurt them in the long run.

BUYING ONLINE

ID: 313

I have never been scammed before (or at least as long as I can remember) until tonight. I was searching for a Flash Website template to buy and came across this simple one I like

http://www.bluegelmedia.com/website-templates/website-templates-type/22742.html

I clicked on the BUY THIS TEMPLATE button and it redirected me to this site for Check Out.

http://www.templatehelp.com/preset/cart.php?act=add&templ=22742&pr_code=ObW1G8SxD3ib3KtUU70gB2i8GZxh0k

I've been shopping online for more than a decade now and I guess I've been lucky until now. I made the payment over PayPal then waited for the email confirmation. Minutes later I got the order confirmation that my transaction went through, but they said I needed to further verify myself by sending a copy of my driver license or passport. I was thinking HELL NO and immediately I knew something's wrong. I went on Google and looked them up and yup they're a scam. From now on, if I'm buying anything online that's not from a well known company/website like eBay, Amazon, Newegg, etc... I will Google their website for fraud/scam reports first. I also learned from my research that scams on Website Templates are huge so be very careful on where you buy/download from.

My Lan T. Tran

HEALTH IS WEALTH

ID: 109

I've always been afraid of doctors. I can still vividly remember the times when my mom almost dragged me every time we went to Dr. Flores' clinic. People in the hospital looked at us with scornful looks due to my wailing until we reached the area, where I got bribed with cholocate-flavoured lollipops.

The same fear still surrounds me now, even at this age (I am 31). Of course, less screaming and dawdling, and candies!

Because of IATROPHOBIA (fear of doctors), I've neglected my health and it brought me some serious health problems – diabetes, hypertension, miscarriage, liver disorders, and all other sorts of stuff.

Recently, my miscarriage, has opened up my eyes to the truth behind "Health is Wealth." Frequent visits to my Ob-Gyn have knocked the irresponsible phobia out of my system. My doctor is really nice, and kind, and though she's been scolding me about not going for health check-ups – I love her!

From this moment on, I am having regular visits to the family doctor. I need to get treated on several disorders, the priority of which is now my diabetes.

Prevention is better than cure, in all instances. I hope it isn't too late for me.

TAKING MY REVENGE WITHOUT IMPUNITY

ID: 483

Because of an unpleasant experience I had with a man, I swore that one day I would take my revenge, and when I did, it should be done without

Mistakes In Life: The Path To Wisdom

impunity. I also decided I would also make somebody fall madly and deeply in love with me and tear him apart. It should be I who has the last laugh. Because of that, I activated an account from a particular social network. I joined dating sites just to find some prey. Fortunately, I found not just one, but three guys.

I did my best to entice them, I let them spend a lot of money to send me gifts and other unnecessary material things, and most of all I demanded them come to my place and meet me. Poor guys, so gullible and stupid enough to obey my commands. Nobody was aware of my plan; they never even suspected my motives. I was so jubilant making these guys miserable, until the day came when the odds turned back at me.

One of these guys became my steady BF, when I knew that he was head-over-heels in love with me, for no reason at all, I broke up with him. I never talked to him, never answered his calls, and blocked him from my social network; just shut him out of my life. I was so happy knowing that he was in complete agony with what I had done.

Until one day I got a call from an unknown number, it was from his mom, telling me that her son was in a coma because after the break-up, he went into a drinking spree. He went home drunk driving, on his way home he was side swiped by a ten wheeler cargo truck. All of them were blaming me; according to them, if I did not break up with him, maybe it wouldn't have happenned. When I tried to visit him at the hospital, I was not allowed to get inside his room.

When I went home a pang of guilt hit me. Somehow, I was responsible for his condition, for that I went to church and prayed. I asked for forgiveness from God and most of all asked God to spare his life. However, a week after being comatose all of his systems failed and finally died. Because of that almost everyone who knew blamed me. I was entirely distraught that time; I was branded a killer, a murderer.

From that time I never got peace of mind, so I decided to stay away from anybody who knew me. I moved and tried to pick up the pieces of the broken fragments of myself. I applied for a new job and started living as a new person trying to shut down all those bad memories. At first it was too hard; but with prayers I finally moved on.

My Lan T. Tran

Lesson: Making someone pay the debts of others is not right because the price you might be paying in return might be greater than what has been owed to you.

GAMBLING

ID: 52

One time I was sent to the store to do some shopping, but on the way I found people standing in a group and I joined them to find out what was happening. That was when I noticed that gambling was taking place. There were three cards with different names written on them and the guy on stage would interchange them and ask a gambler to identify which contained a certain name. Upon identification, the person would win the bet and if they fail they would lose. I found it very easy and I decided to give it a trial, and I bet the money I had been given for shopping. Believe it or not, I won and I got tempted to play again, this time with my cash and what I had won. I was unlucky and I lost everything, I cried and pleaded for a refund because the money did not belong to me but they turned a deaf ear to me. I went home without any of the things I was supposed to be shopping for. I received a good beating and was punished by going hungry for a night. I learned that gambling is not good and if you do gamble, be ready to lose as well. The chances for losing are higher than for winning because it is a business that benefits the owner.

SAY WHAT YOU MEAN

ID: 341

Don't assume that people will understand your intentions. I recently graduated from a university and my parents had planned a trip to Ireland that ran over my graduation ceremony date. I told my mother that it was okay to miss my graduation because I didn't want to be responsible for them not being able to go on their trip. Meanwhile, I was feeling rather hurt that they would rather go to Ireland than see me graduate. I never told them this and instead got upset when it was too late (because they had already booked their trip). The result was a fight between my mom and I. She felt so guilty that she rescheduled her trip and probably ended up paying hundreds of dollars to rebook it. Next time I need to say what I feel before it's too late.

THE WIRELESS BUTTON

ID: 144

I have used a computer almost daily since high school and while that is the extent of experience I have in technology, it does not mean I am bad with technology. In fact I taught technology at a local middle school which is what made this situation so embarrassing. One evening I was working on a paper for one of my online classes when the Internet went out. This happens pretty often so I did not initially think much of it. I went into the other room and reset the router, unplugged the modem, and restarted my computer. This series of actions usually took care of the problem, but not this time. I didn't panic. I called the cable and Internet company and they reset everything though it seemed everything was in working order. I restarted my laptop again to no avail. I started to panic as time was passing and my paper was due that night. All of my work had been saved online and I could not start over, not this late. I spent an hour reinstalling drivers and the modem software. I was on the edge of tears when my ten year old walked over and ask what was wrong. I explained that my school work was due and I could not get the Internet to work. He said, "Can I try?" What could it hurt, I wasn't getting anywhere. He picked up my laptop, looked at it and didn't seem to do anything when he handed it back and said ok I fixed it. I stared in amazement as my Internet was up and running. I grabbed him and hugged him and asked what he did. He smirked and said he pushed the button. I almost fell over when what he said hit me. As I was typing I must have hit the wireless connection button. I never thought to check it. I learned that day to always look for the simplest solution first and if all else fails, ask the kids how to fix the computer.

My Lan T. Tran

KNOW THYSELF

ID: 597

There are so many people who are over confident about themselves. It's not bad to be confident, but it's really bad to be over confident. Once I was over confident, so I really know the disadvantages of being over confident.

I had so much confidence about me that back then I thought I could do anything, there was nothing that I could not do. And that thinking cost me too much. I tried to be something that I was not, and that made my life like a living hell; and I really ended up badly.

I tried to be a politician but to be a perfect politician one thing is very important; you must be a good actor and also you need to know what is happening around you. But I was never fit for this. And that's why my political carrier ended quickly, suddenly and badly.

But now I know I was wrong, as no one can do everything. If everyone can do anything, then we don't need to be in society. We live together because we need one another's help. Everyone has his own expertise about something; no one is an expert in everything. But alas! It was too late for me. So, try to know yourself and don't end up like me.

SLEEPING IN CLASS

ID: 70

During lecture time while I was studying at a university, I would sometimes doze off if the lecture got boring. My friends would wake me up at the end of the lesson. One time, my friends decided to teach me a lesson by not waking me after the lecture was over. So they didn't wake me up, and they left me in the lecture hall after the lesson. I must have slept for over two hours because when I woke up the lecture hall was empty and I was all alone. I quickly went to my room and I learned a lesson. From that day on, I stopped sleeping in class, and I thanked my friends for teaching me that lesson. My advice is that if you are feeling sleepy in class, take a walk or sit next to an open window to keep the sleep away.

Mistakes In Life: The Path To Wisdom

PLAYING GOD

ID: 368

Right before my senior year in college, I got my girlfriend pregnant. Like a lot of people our age, it was the kind of problem everyone dreaded. I had at least a year of school left excluding the board exam review period while she had just graduated from nursing school. Both of us weren't from well off families so this was a nightmare for us. Though I was an only child, she was the eldest of four. People expected her to be the one to support her siblings through high school and college. So I did what was probably the single most stupid mistake of my life — I asked her to have the baby aborted.

This created more problems than it solved. For instance, in a country that hasn't legalized abortion, there is no safe and accepted procedure that will guarantee a woman's health. While I was asking her to go through the procedure, I was unconsciously asking her to risk herself as well. I may have used her responsibility to her family as a reason to do this but we both knew I had my self-interests as well. The whole thing caused a gap between us even while we continued to see each other. The thought of having asked for such an act affected me as well. It caused me to doubt my character as before this, I often prided myself for making sound and balanced decisions. People may not have known the truth but I felt so guilty about it that during those times, I lost all self-confidence.

Luckily, she got me to listen to her and we did all that we could to make things work. The road was never smooth for us; there were a few more occasions where blames were cast and hurtful words were exchanged. But with forgiveness came healing.

I asked her to marry me three years later. It is the best decision I made so far. At present, we're currently raising and enjoying our little boy who seems to erase every little worry away. Who would've thought this was how things would play out?

My Lan T. Tran

TAKING CARE OF MY BABY

ID: 175

My baby nearly fell from our bed yesterday. I gave her a bottle while she was enjoying herself by pushing some pillows using her legs. She really likes doing it with her feet. Kicking and pushing things by using them. After a whole day of taking care of her, I realized I hadn't eaten a decent meal and was suddenly feeling so hungry. So, I went to the kitchen to get myself something to eat for just a few minutes but at the moment I entered the room, she was already at the edge of the bed about to fall. I was petrified but quickly ran to her and grabbed her by the arms. Luckily, I was quick enough to stop her from falling from a three foot high bed,.... however I spilled my plate of cookies onto the floor.

Lesson learned, no more leaving her alone, especially now that she's a crawling and climbing baby. I think babies nowadays are more active than ever. You really have to watch them. It only takes them two seconds to make a move. I try to keep her on the floor and make sure to keep her out of the way of anything dangerous.

I DESERVED THAT PUNISHMENT

ID: 550

When I was a first year varsity student, I was arrogant and selfish. I was also inattentive and I tried to disturb those who were paying attention. Most of my classmates and friends were fed up with that behavior. But they could not say anything, because if they said that, I would disturb them more. But one day I got caught by our hydrology teacher. He was so angry. He threw me out of the class. At that time I thought he was cruel and boring. But later I understood it wasn't him, I was the one who was both cruel and boring. I was destroying not only mine but also my friends' future from my actions in class. Then I took a vow not do it further and I would pay attention in my classes.

Mistakes In Life: The Path To Wisdom

SAY I LOVE YOU, IF YOU HAVE THE CHANCE TO

ID: 218

Before, I didn't know how to express my feelings in words. As far as I could remember, I didn't often say "I love you" or "Take care" aloud. I guess I thought showing it through actions was already enough. However, I found out the importance of it when I met my husband. He is an expressive person. He always says "I love you" whenever he has a chance to. Whenever we're sitting on the couch, eating a meal, before going to sleep and right after we wake up in the morning. Before, I didn't answer his statements as often as he said them but eventually I got used to it and felt the pleasure of the words and responded with the same words every time. Now I always say I love you to my daughter as often as I have the chance to. I realized that it greatly adds to the value of how you are feeling towards the person or how much you value the person. If you do show your love and care in action, the words emphasize and confirm it. It eliminates doubts and confusions. It gives that person being addressed an assurance that the things you do mean the same thing as the things you say. It also gives the feeling of release and relief for being able to tell the person what you dearly feel about him or her.

ADDICTION

ID: 404

Ever since I was born, I've been playing games using any console. At the age of 6, I played any game using the Family Computer Disk System. From then on, I've played a variety of consoles, from Gameboy to PlayStation.

As I aged, the hobby continued to progress; from being a hobby to an addiction. Usually, I only play when I'm bored, but then I incorporated it into my lifestyle. Grades sunk, and I neglected my health. I got to the point where I only ate once a day, just to fulfill my desires to enjoy gaming. My vision blurred, and I grew weaker each day. I lost sight of the goals in life I once had.

I began questioning myself, what do I get from being too addicted to gaming? Nothing. I failed my studies, I failed my parents, and worse, I failed myself. I finally realized that too much of anything in life comes with a price. As I continue to rebuild myself, I tell myself, that having fun is never wrong, as long as I do it with moderation.

I DIDN'T KNOW WHAT TO DO

ID: 568

When I was a student, I used to wear skin tight or body fitted jeans. Although they were not comfortable, I would wear them. One day I went to play football, wearing one of those jeans. It was quite hard to play while wearing these, but I was trying my best to make it work. At one point I got the ball. I ran towards the goal but when I kicked the ball, it didn't go through the goal post and something happened to my pants. I heard a sound, like something was tearing apart. Then I discovered my pants were torn apart and if I walked or ran everyone would see this too. So I could not walk or run, I was standing still like a statue. I didn't know what to do. At last I took a towel from one of my friends and covered it up and then went home. That incident really made me feel ashamed and now I'm afraid to wear body fitting clothes.

FISHY GO BYE BYE

ID: 5

One time, I decided to do my grandmother a favor as a surprise and clean the fish bowl with her fish in it. After I was done I put it on the heater and went to do something else. Later on when I was eating dinner, I noticed that the fish was zipping around in its bowl like crazy. I went over to look at it and noticed the heater was on and it was being cooked alive in its bowl. My mother had come home and turned on the heat without my knowledge. Lesson learned: always put things back where they belong and be careful of where you put things. You could kill something.

Mistakes In Life: The Path To Wisdom

NO TO IMPULSIVE SHOPPING

ID: 94

In one of my previous posts, I gave a story about losing my Kindle on a plane. By now, you can probably see how I really loved my Kindle because I am posting another story about it.

Because I kept on whining about how I missed it and about how disappointed I was on losing it, my husband got so tired of me that he asked me to purchase one and have it delivered a.s.a.p. I must admit that I got excited about it, but on the other hand was hesitant because of an additional expense that wasn't really needed at all. I thought about it for around a month or two, until the "money-conscious" spender in me gave up and started browsing online at www.amazon.com for Kindle offers. The original price of this gadget was $189 but surprisingly, it was being offered at $139. I called my husband right away and asked if I could order it. He was surprised that I hadn't done so since he had already told me to several weeks ago. Without giving much thought, I clicked on ORDER and CHECKOUT. The total cost went up to $180 because I also ordered a lighted leather case for it. End of deal – I was happy.

The next day, I received an SMS from my officemate that said – "THREE NEW KINDLES OUT!!!" I didn't get it at first, until, when I logged onto Amazon to get the status of my order... I saw THREE NEW KINDLE "TOUCH" units on my screen. They just launched it that same day!!! I must admit that I felt awful, for not even waiting for just a day more! Well who would have known, right? The more disheartening news was that the cheapest new Kindle, that has a "touch" screen only cost $79. I can't describe the details anymore, I still feel bad about my "rush shopping."

While the Kindle I bought wasn't really bad and still really serves it purpose for me, I could have gotten a better deal if I had researched more. I'm pretty sure some news had already leaked on the internet about these gadgets, but I hadn't bothered to do some research.

This experience, again, taught me – Google is your friend, research! And... NO TO IMPULSIVE BUYING. Make sure to do the proper fact-finding and "window-shopping" before buying anything.

My Lan T. Tran

NEVER MAKE A PROMISE YOU CAN'T KEEP

ID: 451

I always tried to please people even when I did not prepare to think about what they would expect from me. But this cliché is always true – never make a promise when you can't keep it. One day one of my friends was throwing her 18th birthday and in an effort to save some money, she asked me whether I could do her a favor. I said yes right away to her simple request of having to make all her giveaways. I thought they were easy to make as long as she had all the resources. It was months since she had asked me and I was anxious with the fact that my friend's birthday was only a few weeks away. Although I started a few bits and was able to show her that I did finish a few, the job could not be finished on the time she was expecting because I was singlehandedly making all the giveaways. Of course, it was pro bono but I did not mind. But then I became too stressed out with the job and my brother noticed me losing sleep. Luckily he was more creative than I was and helped me out with the project. I did most of the finishing touches and most of the base for the giveaways my brother handled so well. Good thing my friend's birthday was successful and she was happy, but my health suffered in the process. And two things I learned from this situation were: never try to please anyone and never make a promise just to please them. Your friend might get hurt if you turned them down, but you are only doing yourself and them a favor. The most important thing I learned was to be more honest with myself and to try to say 'no' when I know I am not really capable of doing something.

MY NEIGHBOR DOESN'T CARE

ID: 259

I moved into a new apartment a year ago and one of the unfortunate things that happened was hearing my downstairs neighbor playing his music really loud. It's so loud you could feel the bass. I didn't mind it at first because I thought maybe he did not know someone already moved to the apartment. However, it has not gotten any better, he plays his loud music when he comes home everyday and then keeps it up most nights. I have told our landlord, however it has done nothing to stop the neighbor's music every day. I have a shifting work schedule and the loud music has really made it very difficult to sleep. So one day, I went to his room and asked him if he could lower the volume, however, he never said anything, walked away and played his music even louder than ever at times. He is just plain rude. After a couple of months, I moved to another place. I surveyed that new area first and made sure I would get nicer neighbors. Now, before I move to another apartment or room, I ask questions to the current or previous tenants first to know what the area is like, so that I don't have that kind of neighbor anymore.

FOLLOWING YOUR DREAMS

ID: 598

Growing up builds ones' dreams of so many things depending on what they come in contact with. Somehow the specific things we want to do when we grow up tend to disappear as new things take our interest and we set sail for that direction.

I have had such an experience and ended up doing what seemed to bring money and moved my focus from what really made me happy. It is only when you have set sail and reached a storm that realization sets in that the wrong path must have been taken.

For me, it was picking up courses that I was convinced was in the market and I let the decision be made for me. I took up the classes for a year and in each semester I failed so badly. This course of action was not taken kindly by my parents as they believed they were building my future and I was out to ruin it all. My degree was literally picked for me and the university and where I would stay and where I would work once I finished.

I struggled so much trying to explain to my parents that I did not want that path but the problem was that when asked what I wanted, I went silent. I also did not know. I did assessments on my own and tried reading on different careers and then it occurred to me that I could simply start small in the interests I had. From fashion to business to events, I took every scenario and immersed myself.

My lesson has come at a heavy price after so much money has been spent but realizing what I can easily do and enjoy has finally come and it makes me happy that I engage in the things I dreamt of as a child and literally living the dreams I had built years ago.

STAYING BACK

ID: 32

This year is my sophomore year in high school. If I had done any worse in school I would've had to stay back. Going into high school, I didn't know what was waiting for me. So I spent that time fooling around, instead of studying. Then came my final report card. I didn't do so well. I had failed four classes. In order for me not to stay back, I had to go and attend summer school. Since I was only able to take two sessions in summer school, I decided to take the important classes, English and math. Later on during my summer, a letter from my school said that all 9th grade students were to report to school in full uniform on the 25th. In that letter, I was not able to find my 10th grade schedule, so I didn't know what to do. Thus, I had decided not to go that day. My first day of school I went in and asked for my schedule. The principal said that it had not come in the mail because they had to change my schedule in order for me to graduate. So now I have no study hall and two history classes. The lesson here is take your time in school, to study. If you do well in school, you will have plenty of time to fool around later on in your life.

IT'S THAT SMOKE

ID: 316

I experienced loss of appetite a few years ago, got very sick, followed by dramatic weight loss because of too much smoking. I was skin and bones. I

Mistakes In Life: The Path To Wisdom

remembered finishing 3 cigarettes' packs a day. Still I didn't think I had a problem. Friends and families had advised me to stop this vice or even just minimize it but I was oblivious of them. The final toll had occurred when I was rushed to the hospital for unstoppable coughing and terrible chest pain. I was diagnosed with lung complications and firmly advised by my Doctor that another stick could kill me. After being confined for more or less a month in the hospital, being forced to take all those medicines and having incredible chest pain, I finally decided not to go back to smoking. But it was a very long and tedious process. Because I was considered a cigarette addict, I had to undergo therapy and classes to finally quit smoking. I also needed the firm support of my family and friends. I had to stay away from my smoking friends to not be tempted or asked them to not smoke around me.

Just a piece of advice, don't wait for that moment where you have to undergo terrible pain or ruin a part of your life before you quit smoking.

BE CAREFUL WHEN IT'S WET

ID: 111

There was this one instance during my high school days that I can't forget. It was when I slipped and got embarrassed because everybody saw me. It was one rainy day when the hallway was wet because of the non-stop rain. It was break time and most of my classmates and schoolmates were hanging out along the hallway stalls. I was on my way to the library and had to pass that hallway. I remembered that I was kind of in a hurry that time and that I was not cautious of the wet lane. Then the unexpected happened. While walking in the middle of the hallway, I suddenly slipped and fell on my butt. It didn't hurt much but I think all the stares and laughter from my schoolmates hurt more. It only happened once but after that day whenever I passed a group of people, I would overhear them laughing and saying "that's the lame girl, who slipped."

That event had taught me to always be careful with my actions. Always look at the path I am walking on. Don't be over confident when walking in a wet pathway because you might slip and worst you might get hurt badly.

My Lan T. Tran

LESSONS FROM THE CURSE OF DIMINUTIVE KNOWLEDGE

ID: 484

When I was studying in my undergraduate level, I was studying a course called Investment theory where I was assigned to a practical work of maintaining a portfolio in our Share Market. I did that for 2 months and dramatically I made a profit percentage of 70% within these two months. How did I do this? I did not know. But from gathering this knowledge, I jumped into having my business life without proper study of the overall market though my teacher advised me to be patient for few more months. That greed eventually made me come up with a net loss of 50% only within the third month of my business. That is because when I entered into the market, the market was inflated enough to collapse at any time. I lost most of my money (which I gathered through very hard work) and got a lesson from Excessive greed and impatience.

SUFFERING

ID: 53

I was clearing the chicken coop one day and accidentally hit a chicken with the shovel by mistake and it died. I knew my mother would be very angry and so I decided not to report the matter. I thought no one had seen me, so I quickly buried the chicken and I thought nobody would ever know it was I who killed it. Unfortunately, our baby sitter was watching me the whole time. When I went into the house, she told me that she had seen what I had done. I pleaded with her not tell my mom and she agreed, but on the condition that I would do whatever she wanted me to do. The baby sitter would demand that I always clean the dishes and carry out some of her duties. Whenever I declined, she threatened to tell my mum. After submitting to her for a long time, I gave up on her demands and decided to tell my mom because the duties were too much on me. When I told my mom, she didn't even beat me! She just said it was okay and I should be careful next time. I learned that it's good to report any damage instead of suffering silently and that there is no need to be afraid.

Mistakes In Life: The Path To Wisdom

PEOPLE AREN'T ALWAYS WHAT THEY SEEM

ID: 342

When I first met my friend Jen, I didn't like her at all. I had gone out with a few friends to have a couple drinks at a small local bar, and Jen was there. She was loud, and over the top and at the time I thought she was completely obnoxious. I decided that first night that I didn't like her and was never going to. Every time I saw her, I created excuses in my head to avoid getting to know her, and admitting that she might just be having fun. Then one night, she had come out to see a band that I was seeing. We ended up chatting that night, and later ended up dancing and having a great time. We have been great friends ever since. I realized that night that we first got to know each other, that maybe I hadn't judged her fairly that first night. I have decided that in the future it is probably best not to judge people before I get a chance to spend a little time with them, because who knows what I might be missing.

BE SENSITIVE TO YOUR EMPLOYEES – PART 1

ID: 137

Employee #1 – your driver.

We've had our driver for more than a year now. He was a former cab driver whose services we often availed of when we needed transport, and as soon as we got ourselves a car, we immediately thought about hiring him permanently to work for us.

On his first year with us, we concluded there was no doubt we made the right decision hiring him. We went along very well with him. Though he drives really crazy most of the time, he gives us consolation through the fact that we get to- and out of- work really early even with traffic. Everything was running smoothly, until... around three months ago, he was acting really strange, and most of all annoying! He ignored us when we talked to him – as if he didn't hear anything; his driving was erratic; he was always late; he got grumpy when we had to keep him until the late evening; he didn't eat the food we gave him; and he did not turn up to work for several days. He became the exact opposite of the ideal driver we knew him to be.

I have contemplated on firing him and I have almost done so, more than ten times now. It is only the fact that he has an adopted kid, – a girl who is four years old – that he needs to take care of. I couldn't be burdened by guilt should something miserable happen to his daughter.

Anyway, I let things be because of the pity I have for his kid. Though he sometimes ruins my day, I still just let his attitude pass by. I am on the verge of firing him though.

Surprisingly one day, when he had "alone time" with my husband, (they had to go to an auto shop whose owner is my husband's friend), he started opening up. He was having these financial problems with his partner – the girl sold their house, the money is gone, without him knowing. Aside from being homeless soon, he has to send his daughter to the province for assurance of the three basic needs – food, clothing, shelter. He said some other things that bothered him, and eventually he said sorry that his mood swings seemed to have really affected the way I act towards him. Wow – talk about guy talk!

As soon as we got home, my husband told me about this, and it just really struck me that I have been so insensitive of his issues. Why didn't I even think about the probability that our driver is probably problematic, thus the attitude? Why didn't I attempt to talk to him? Why didn't I encourage him to let us know if he had issues? I realized it was unfair for me to have judged him negatively without the facts. I realized that we had not been very helpful to him. My friends and relatives used to tell me that "he is just in my payroll" so I can always fire him, however, what I learned today made me think – what if I were in his shoes (not as a driver) as an employee, who does not only have work, but a life outside of it? I thought – if I had personal problems and it affected me at work, would I be okay if my boss fired me too?

Mistakes In Life: The Path To Wisdom

The story seems really odd as I am writing about my driver, but one key thing I want to point out is that "If you want others to be happy, practice compassion. If you want to be happy, practice compassion."

EMBARRASSING EXPERIENCE

ID: 513

Every one of us has had their own embarrassing experience. Well, mine happened when I was in elementary school. I was in grade four at that time. Our teacher gave us a reading activity. Each one of us must stand up and read the words that were being written on the board. While others were reading one by one, me and my seatmate were busy doing some chitchat, we did not notice that it was already our turn to read the words. It took us a second before we realize that all of my classmates were staring on us, still neither one of us had the courage to stand up because we felt so embarrassed and my teacher was already angry. "Awkward" that's the first word that comes to my mind. Then our teacher said something to me that really hurt my feelings. She said that I was the only person she knew who was very dumb and a fool in class, not to mention that my mother was also a teacher. I knew it was my fault. But then, as time passed, those mean words became my inspiration. I finished my studies and proved to myself that I wasn't a fool as my teacher in elementary school said. I learned that I should not let others ruin my life; instead take them as a challenge in your life to pursue your dreams.

PURPLE GRAPE

ID: 71

As a child I would watch TV and see people throwing food up into the air only to catch in their mouths. So I started talking to my brother, and said it would be funny if they ended up choking. Well it just so happened that my grandmother gave my brother and I, a bowl full of grapes. So I tried throwing it up into the air, and catching it in my mouth. It took me a couple of tries, but around the 4th try I had succeeded. I caught in my mouth, but karma just happened to be right around the corner, so I ended up choking on the grape. Lesson learned, karma is a pain in the ass, so make sure you don't do anything stupid like throw food into your mouth. OR try and make assumptions of what might happen to other people because it might just happen to you.

NOT MAIL

ID: 385

My aunts and uncles were all working abroad when I was a kid of 3; most of their kids were also left in the care of my mother. It was chaotic but really fun. Among them I was the youngest, so I had a nanny keep me company at home when they all went to school. Receiving letters from my relatives abroad became a routine in our household, so much so that even at that young age I already realized what they meant when they all came rushing outside at the word, "Mail!".

One day as I was left outside to play, I had a sudden urge to go to the potty. But seeing as it was too far and rather inconvenient, I was left to consider another tactic. I screamed at the top of my lungs, "MAIIIIIIIILLLL!!!" Out came my nanny, rushing to meet the mailman, but there she found me all messy and grinning at her awkwardly. Years later my nanny would recount that day to my utter embarrassment. Lesson learned too late: never do things that will get you embarrassed in the future.

ALWAYS CHECK TWICE

ID: 176

When I was in my teenage years I was very active. My favorite activity was horseback riding and it was a daily adventure. I spent evenings riding and grooming and weekends in the summer showing all over the state. I loved my horse and she had become my best friend at a very tough time in my life. The stables were my get away. I had a trainer that helped me learn the basics and then turned me loose to learn things the hard way. I spent a great deal of time on the ground and I swear my horse laughed at me. The one lesson I truly learned that first year was to always check twice. My trainer taught that the first day, but I never seemed to remember until on overly hot summer afternoon. I was on my horse trotting toward a jump when all of the sudden my saddle started slipping. I didn't know what to do so I tried to pull the horse to a stop which meant that she stopped but the saddle and I did not. As I was falling toward the ground with my saddle the only thought I had was, "I guess I should have double checked that cinch." Never again did I start a ride without double checking my saddle. I will admit that I still hit the ground many times while learning to ride, but never again did my saddle go with me on the trip.

LOSING TIME

ID: 551

There is a quote by Helen Keller that goes "When one door of happiness closes, another opens; but often we look so long at the closed door that we do not see the one which has been opened for us." I can't tell you how many times I made this mistake and how many years of my life were wasted "waiting" and "hoping" for something (someone) that never came (back). Recently, I decided to move on and it's one of the greatest feelings in the world to be able to cut loose from whatever that was holding me back & making me miserable all this time. Ever since I opened my heart again and welcomed whatever the universe decided to send my way, lots of great opportunities and people have come into my life. If any of you readers are on the same boat as I was, please learn from me and just say goodbye to everything and anything that doesn't make you happy. You really can move forward. All you have to do is get yourself to "want" to make that change. "Life is too short to be anything but happy!"

My Lan T. Tran

RESISTING THE URGE TO USE MY CELL PHONE IN A FOREIGN COUNTRY

ID: 220

I just couldn't resist. When I went to Mexico about 10 years ago I had only had my cell phone for a few months and didn't realize that the long distance charges were dramatically different when compared to calling from a landline. Besides – I still lived at home and my parents always paid the long distance bill! When I went to Mexico I phoned home several times because I was homesick. Each time, my mom said "this is going to cost a fortune" and I chose to continue calling her and my friend. I don't know how long each conversation lasted but, based on my bill, there were 11 calls in total. 11 calls and $560 in total – which was almost the entire cost of my trip. Whatever you do, don't call Canada from Mexico on your cell phone! Before you travel, buy pre-paid calling cards. It took me over 3 months to pay that cell phone bill with my low-paying part-time job.

MY EMBARRASSING MOMENT

ID: 406

I was so drunk when I went to class one time. My teacher asked me what happened because I was so dizzy and looked very tired. My teacher went near me and smelled alcohol. I was really embarrassed and then he sent me to the principal's office. I don't want anything like that to happen again because it was really an embarrassing moment. If I ever drink too much alcohol, I will certainly make sure that there is no class on the following day. In order for you to prevent any embarrassing moment in your life, you must make sure that you are aware of everything you do.

DECIDE YOURSELF

ID: 570

I remember a time when I was in the twelfth grade. It was a year that I prepared for the national exam. I was really working hard to score good results. Day and night I studied for long hours and my friends were also preparing. Then the time came. We all had completed our preparation and after a couple days we took the national exam. The exam was very nice and I scored top points. The adventure started at this period when I was selecting a field of study and university. At that time my friends and I were filling out the selection form. I wanted to study 'medicine' in a well-known university of my country. Nevertheless, my friends psychologically forced me to change my decision and told me to fill in the same fields as they wanted. They also said to me that 'medicine' was not the best field of study, & they supported the field 'Engineering'. I never tried to oppose them but I supported them and on paper I chose 'Engineering'. After some time, the field that I had selected was available and I got 'Engineering' in a university that I don't want to learn. At that moment, I felt very sad and blamed myself for changing my decision. This part of my life reminds me that I may ask for someone's consultations but whatever decision I make, I will not give a single space of intervention of other ideas into my life, period!

I SHOULD HAVE GRABBED IT...

ID: 6

I must have been about 19 or 20, and to this day I still remember what the painting looked like. I have been to many yard sales, estate sales and flea markets before. I have seen the odd the unique and unusual. Every once in a while I would find something that really struck me in a way that evoked some sort of indescribable emotion in me, and I knew that I just had to buy it...

On this particular day, I scoured through old and torn boxes for that something special. I sifted through the unwanted items and tokens from a person's front yard. As I looked through a pile of old prints and paintings with some broken and whole frames, I saw something. It was a simple original painting that struck a chord in my heart and I fell in love with it. I was in a rush that day, so I put the picture in the back and figured I would come back later for it.

When I came back of course, I realized that someone else had already purchased it. To this day I still have hope that I might see it again, even though the chances are slim. I did learn a valuable lesson. When you see something that you want... just get it if you can... because if you don't, it will probably be gone by the time you come back for it...

SNARING A GUY

ID: 95

I was 20, and for some reason, I wanted to marry and quickly settle down. I met a young guy, fell in love, and decided to treat him well, so he'd really love me back. My mistake was letting him think that I liked giving massages. I hate giving massages. Well, out of love and habit I am still massaging him after 23 years, and he has come to expect it and he acts like a baby if I say 'no'. What I have learned is that it was a mistake, not the marriage, but by offering him a token that he came to believe was his due. Be yourself, don't change to make someone like you or love you. I learned my lesson the hard way, and I hope I can stop some folks from making a similar mistake.

TAKE TIME

ID: 453

I grew up with my grandmother and she became my best friend. We were really close and we really cared for each other. My grandmother's death really made me feel so guilty because I failed to visit her while she was still in the hospital because of my studies. I hated myself because I did not even think that it would be the last time that I would see her alive. I never got a chance to said thank you to her. I was really wrong in making my decision. From the scenario, I realized that it would be better to be absent in my class than not to visit my loved ones in the hospital because I am quite sure that it would be the best thing to do at the moment. We must take time to visit a friend or our love ones in times of sorrow and need, like when they are ill because this is really the time that they need us most.

DON'T GOSSIP

ID: 265

Earlier this year, I hated a classmate with a passion. She was my main topic of conversation most of the time. We used to be best friends too, so I knew a lot about her. Her ex boyfriend, also hated/s her, so we would talk about her a lot. One time, I told him about how she had sex with her current boyfriend, and he flipped out. He was screaming at her and calling her a slut, then told the whole school. Now, I regret telling him this because now she doesn't have any true friends anymore. They all started to flip out on her because I started it first. To repay her, I'm trying to be her friend, but it's really hard to be nice to someone you don't like. Lesson learned, don't gossip. It's very bad.

JOB SCAM

ID: 599

Desperate situations can really bring the ugly side of ourselves and mine came out when I was conned out of my money. It was one of those times, jobs were not coming in and there was no cash flow and the responsibilities were piling up. There was an advertisement of a job application that seemed to suit my qualifications and I set out to find out more about the company.

All details were given and I decided to press on with sending my credentials. I was called in for an interview and I was requested to send some money using a mobile service because they wanted to cater for my application process plus transport to and from the company. It looked genuine although very fishy and I still sent out the money and was told when and where I would pick up the bus that would drive the applicants to the said venue for vetting.

On the set date, I went ahead and waited at the said place. The expected bus never came and worse of all the phone lines did not go through. I later realized we were many people all waiting for the same said bus and on comparing notes it became all too clear we had been conned.

The biggest lesson is to be wary of job scams which pry on individuals desperate to get a livelihood.

PUNCH BUGGY
ID: 33

There was a point in time where I thought punch buggy was fun. So every time I saw one, I would punch everyone lightly and say no punch backs! One day I punched my aunt. My aunt was driving, so she couldn't take her eyes off the road, but she still punched me back, but instead of on the arm, it was a big smack on my lips. It didn't exactly hurt, but it felt numb, then it felt like a cold sore! My aunt started laughing at me so much while saying sorry, but I didn't know why until I looked in the mirror and saw my lips were HUGE!!! I never played punch buggy again.

OY, WHY DOES THIS LOTION BURN
ID: 318

Not too long ago, I was in a hurry to go out and play in the sun for hours that I accidentally grabbed the Thera-Gesic pain relieving cream maximum strength instead of the sun block lotion and put a ton of it on my right leg. The funny thing is the two tubes don't even look the same. They also have different smell. My mind was too busy thinking about other things that I didn't realize I used the wrong one until my right leg was burning up HOT HOT HOT! I had to quickly wash it off, but it still remained red for quite a while. Lesson learned here is to be more aware of what you're doing and sometimes trying to speed things up will only slow it down even more. Take time to do things right the first time around.

DON'T HOLD THEM DOWN

ID: 113

I am by no means a beautician and unfortunately my daughter found that out at an early age. I thought she would look cute with bangs, and I decided it would not be that hard and I could cut them. I had always trimmed the ends of her long hair and we had had no major accidents, so how hard could it be? I combed out her hair and decided how far back the bangs should go and began cutting. The first few cuts looked great. Her bangs were straight, but still too long. So once again I got out the spray bottle and soaked her hair and combed out the now shortened locks. I then placed my hand on the bang area and started straightening and shortening to the appropriate length. What I forgot to account for was that when I removed my hand the hair would bounce back up. My daughter suddenly had bangs that were only a couple inches long and sat much too high on her forehead. I learned that day that haircuts, especially big changes, should probably best be left to the professionals. My daughter wore many cute hats and scarves for the next few weeks, but we all survived the first and last time Mommy cut bangs.

ONE MORE CHANCE

ID: 448

I entered college with one goal in mind, to graduate and to become successful one day. It started great, but then it all went wrong.

My Lan T. Tran

Being in a new environment, choosing friends is definitely risky. I was one of those who unluckily got the wrong ones. First semester started, and I was so hyped up with all the things I would learn from school. I got high grades, and I was so happy that I could make my parents proud. Then, it got to the point when I got so pressured to keep up my grades; it stressed me out. I worked hard, depriving myself of the fun I could have had like other people my age. I started going out, partying all night, and in turn, failing my grades. For 4 years, I lied to my dad who was working abroad.

The time came when my dad found out, he was so mad, not about how I led my life, but because of how I neglected all his care for me. He wanted me to be happy, and after all those years, he never had stopped me from having fun. All he wanted was for me to graduate with good grades, and appreciate his efforts. I was so ashamed of myself that I wanted to die. But I realized, continuing to be depressed about everything wouldn't make up for everything I had done. I transferred to another school, and started a new life.

Life is short; appreciate all the love and care given by people who care for you. It's never too late to change for the better, after all, everybody deserves a second chance.

VALUE OF A MOTHER

ID: 54

Whenever my mother sent me to get something for her, I would complain and even refuse to go. Sometimes I would get a beating and my mom would comment, "when you get your own child you will know the pain of motherhood". I didn't take it seriously and after many years passed, I had my own child and the process was so painful that I remembered the words of my mother. Whenever I asked my son to do something and he disobeyed or answered rudely to me, I got very bitter because I remembered the pain I felt. I have learned that life is like an echo and whatever you do will be done unto you. It is good to obey our parents because they sacrifice a lot for children.

Mistakes In Life: The Path To Wisdom

HUMILITY AT WORK

ID: 343

My last job was a total pain, indeed it caused me more sleepless nights than any other depressing thoughts I used to have. Of course there was a reason behind this: my boss. Now my boss isn't unkind, she's not the type you would curse to hell for being evil or inconsiderate. But even though she treated me humanely enough, she did not seem to be logical and relied on her emotions too much. In the back of my head I would mutter to myself, "Yes, what would you expect from a lady boss?" This thinking bothered me throughout the time I spent on my job, until finally I decided to quit. My other workmates tried to talk me out of it, but I could not see why I should answer to a cry-baby boss. So after two years on the job, I quit.

Later on I had a real hard time trying to look for employment. I could not understand why no one would want to hire me. So I took a step back to evaluate myself realistically. For one, I liked my old job. My boss, though she was pretty emotional and sometimes illogical, did treat me better than most of my friends' bosses whenever the topic would come up in our conversations. "Well, therein lies the mistake you made, and you have to be mature in facing the consequences of that decision", my mother said to me when I came complaining to her.

The lesson here is quite simple: always be humble, it pays if you worked hard and did it diligently. Don't think that you're better than your boss; after all they were promoted to that position because they can do the job. And if you really are thinking of quitting your job, always evaluate where you are in your life right now. When I quit my job, I did not realize that the money I saved was only enough to get me through a year or so. In this kind of economy, it always pays to stick it through a difficult time.

HOW MY BABY GOT DIAPER RASHES

ID: 148

I am a first time mom of a 10 month old baby and I admit being a mom is a lot of work. There was a time where I wasn't really sure on how often I should change my baby's diaper. I used both cloth and disposable diapers. During the day I do 'cloth diapering' and disposable ones at night for uninterrupted sleep. I normally change the cloth diapers 4-5 times during the day. However, at night I thought I would only use one diaper for the entire time that my baby was asleep. I kept on doing this for several days until I noticed red small rashes on my baby's behind. I was told that it was diaper rashes and was advised not to leave the wet diaper for so long. The pediatrician prescribed a sort of cream and baby powder to get rid of the rashes and luckily it was eventually healed.

After that experience, I made sure not to leave the wet diaper for more than an hour or so and change it right away if I smell poop. My baby hasn't got any rashes anymore.

NEVER BREAK HEARTS

ID: 514

Love is a gift of nature. Everyone falls in love, some once in lifetime, others several times. As I remember, I was none of them. Once, love was like a game to me. I flattered several girls, had sex but never fell in love with anyone, until I met Arshi. It was March 27, 2010, the day of orientation of first years at our campus. For being one of the celebrated and senior students, I had to attend the function. There I met Arshi, one of the newcomers. My friend introduced me to her. She was beautiful, but not the type who could cause distraction. After getting introduced I met her again, alone and asked her for lunch. She declined but gave me her cell phone number. I never thought this was going to change my life.

That night I called her and we talked for about 2 or 3 hours. About a month later she fell in love with me, but as she was very shy, she could not tell me. From my previous experience with girls, soon I caught her, asked her out and she said yes.

Although I was not, she was so serious about our affair. We used to hang out, walk by the river and look at one another's eyes. As she was very conservative, it took me three months to kiss her for the first time. When I kissed her, I realized that she is the one and only girl whom I have ever loved. After that, I became so serious and told her everything about myself. But that was the great mistake of my life.

After knowing the truth about my past, she said only one thing "I hate you". And that was the last word I heard from her. I tried to call her cell, but she didn't answer. I wanted to talk to her, face to face, but she wouldn't. For about a month I tried so hard just to talk to her once. Every step I took ended with great failure and made me a cheap man to her.

Then suddenly I understood that nature was taking revenge on me. I realized what I did to the other girls, who loved me. I dumped all of them without any reason. And now nature is taking revenge for my deeds. At that time I made myself a promise; I would never ever play with anyone's heart. Because now I know, when a heart is broken, no one can see. But whoever's heart breaks.... only he/ she will know how it feels.

So please don't play with anyone's heart. If you play with anyone's heart, someday someone else will do the same to you.

KEEPING TIME

ID: 72

I had a habit of arriving late for my appointments for no apparent reason even when I woke early. One time I was going to the airport, and as usual I got there late by a few minutes because there was a very bad traffic jam. When I got into departures, the plane's doors had already been closed and I could not board the flight. I had to wait for another flight, pay a fine and I had to travel late at night. I arrived late at night and the person who was waiting for me had given-up and also left. I got stranded at the airport in a foreign country but I managed to take a taxi. I learned to manage time because it can cost you money and cause inconvenience for others.

My Lan T. Tran

KNOW YOUR OWN LIMITS

ID: 378

I had a nice apartment with a friend one year because we both had really good jobs and were able to afford something bigger and nicer. We used to throw parties for our friends, nothing too crazy but a lot of laughing and joking and having a great time. At that time I used to drink to keep up with people, I would try and drink like my guy friends and end up sick. Sometimes when I woke up in the morning I would lay there hiding my head under my blankets wondering what I had said and done the night before. After a while I learned that I don't need to keep up with anyone, I need to know my own limits so that I can have a good time. After these experiences, I have started having a much better time, because I am not trying to impress anyone, and instead I'm just enjoying what my body can handle.

REVIEW YOUR ANSWERS BEFORE SUBMITTING THEM

ID: 183

I applied for a job once, passed the initial interview and took an online simulation exam. It was a time-limiting online exam. The facilitator clearly explained that we need to review our answers before submitting it, because we can only go on to the second phase interview if we passed the 1st level test. So I did try my very best to answer the questions correctly and sensibly. It was composed of essay questions to test our communication skills and transcription sections to assess our listening abilities. I admit that it was a relatively hard and challenging test but as far as I knew and felt I could have passed the test. I did review my answers once and knew that I still had time to go over with the questions again. However, there were some instructions that I didn't clearly understand and didn't dare to read them more than twice, being too conscious that the time was nearing to the specified limit. In short, I decided to pass my answers 10 minutes before the cut-off time without clearly understanding some of the questions and knowing how to answer them. I was fairly

Mistakes In Life: The Path To Wisdom

confident that I would make it. Unfortunately, when the results were announced, my score was 2 points short of the passing score. Yes, I was one of those who left first from the test phases. I know it's a careless move to not review the questions thoroughly; I could have passed the test if only I had reviewed within the 10 minutes of time leftover and tried to answer correctly. My heedlessness cost me a job!

So please review your answers more than twice if possible to make sure you did things right.

I WISH I HAD TALKED TO HIM
ID: 553

Simon was one of my best friends. He was the closest person to me. One year ago he died in an automobile accident. The day before he died, we had a fight. The fight was started because of a misunderstanding. After the fight, when he learned the actual matter, he came to me. But I was so angry that I didn't talk to him. Rather I misbehaved with him. But he didn't say anything rough to me. And that was the last time I saw him. The next day I heard, he was dead. His body was crushed under a truck. I couldn't control my tears. All I could think about was that if I could have known, I would have talked to him. I could have talked to him once more, hug him once more. But he is no longer alive to hug me again.

WATCH OUT FOR THAT BAD AIR!
ID: 223

I know too well that it's a no no to fart in an air conditioned room. However, like others, there are inevitable instances where you can't stop yourself from farting in public because the act simply just goes involuntarily. No matter how much you keep yourself from doing it, it will suddenly and secretly explode. I had learned the importance of restraint one instance when I rode in a carpool with acquaintances on my way to work. I remember eating nothing that early morning but fried eggs and a cup of chocolate drink. While inside the van, I could feel my stomach rumbling from the food I ate, worst part was it was so loud that I knew the people beside me could hear it. The carpool was a little crowded that day and we were sitting close beside each other, so even a penny movement and little noise could be noticed and heard by someone next to you. Believe me I did my best to stop that explosion but it only made the growl in my stomach noisier and made me want to fart even more. So because I couldn't control it anymore and because we were in the middle of the highway, which meant there was no way for me to get out of the van immediately, I did it... just hoping it would be as quiet as possible so that it wouldn't attract the crowd's attention. You see, it did not go the way I wanted. Instead it captured not only the attention of the ones sitting beside me but the entire car. Almost everyone heard the big fart but only a few of them knew who did it. Because we were very close to each other and in a compact van, everyone knew eventually. That wasn't only the worst part; can you imagine that rotten egg smell in the air. That incident made me quit my daily carpool. I couldn't bring myself to face that same crowd again. It took me 3 weeks to find a new carpool service for work.

After that, I made sure to stay away from eggs and hot chocolate as much as possible. If I want to eat eggs, I make sure to pair it with bread or not to drink any chocolate at all.

GETTING OVER A FRIENDSHIP BREAK UP

ID: 407

In my college years, I hung out with people that I thought were my friends. I have my own set of requirements for being a friend and for someone to become a close friend of mine. For me, they should be someone that knows my secrets and be able to keep them, never judgmental for my behaviors regardless, and offer me support when I am going through a phase in my life. In the same way, I would conduct a supportive role for my friends, too. I would never let them down, would constantly give favors, and shower them with affection and undivided time. However, I had

Mistakes In Life: The Path To Wisdom

reached a point in my life where I realized that some of my friends were actually disregarding me and I felt that they were just treating me as a doormat. Doormat is a very demeaning word but I will use it because that is exactly how I felt like from the way they were treating me.

Living with them in the past I remember that they would ask me to buy this, pick something up, do this for them, etc. But when the time came where I would need them, they were all too busy or with their families. Being an unmarried person at the moment, I think I can believe that they are truthfully busy. I tried to distance myself from them for a while and just made a reflection about my relationship with them. They never really reached out and I was not surprised anymore that nobody remembered me. So I tried to immerse myself at work and changed my perspective that some friendships inevitably have to end.

I am still learning the lesson of having to keep moving on and living my own life now rather than playing the role of the victim/martyr, because for all I know they were actually more than happy to get rid of me.

BELIEVE IN YOURSELF

ID: 572

When I was much younger I was expected to do my national exams in high school. I was what you would call someone who had no self confidence. It had been broken over the previous years with constant failing in exams even though I had been selected to join one of the most prestigious schools in the country. I kept using the same formula that brought me to that school but it seemed the harder I tried, the harder I failed.

My ranking dropped so much that my friends were concerned about my grades. The teachers did not make the situation any better with constant reminders of the failures. And to my parents, I was a total disaster. I knew deep down I could perform given a chance to prepare well and being surrounded by positive vibrations. It was hard but I had to let go of a few friends who were not helping my situation and locked myself away from the world including my family for a while all in an attempt to prove I could do it.

It took months but before I knew it, there was a change of tone in the teachers and the friends I had surrounded myself with. They were actually rooting for my success. For the longest time I thought nobody was even paying attention to me. And my family came to understand I needed the concentration and they allowed me my space.

The examinations were done and I actually felt I had done my best because I had given it my all. Months later, the results were out and I had shockingly excelled so well to get selected to a university in my hometown. I was ecstatic about this and my family was very supportive. The teachers hugged with so much joy and they kept saying-all you had to do was believe you could do it and you did just that.

On reflecting, I realized the mistake I had done years before was believing everything I was told by my teachers, friends and family that I was not as good as I thought and I had let it get to me to the extent of believing them. It took a big mind shift and I knew that I had to keep believing in myself to achieve what I had set out to do.

LOST LOVE

ID: 8

One time I went shopping on a business trip and spotted the most beautiful, classy, stylish white coat I had ever seen. I really wanted to buy it, but the price tag stopped me. It wasn't too ridiculously expensive, but definitely something I had never spent that much money on before. After more than half an hour of going back and forth, I decided not to buy it. That was a big mistake. After 6 years I still wish I had bought it. That coat outlived all the people I had ever said "I love you" to, in my memory, lol. Ladies, if you're not a shopaholic, and if once every few years you spot a piece of clothing that melts your heart upon first sight, and if your credit card can afford it, BUY IT! You can always make more money, but you can't turn back time. And if it turns out to be something you don't really like, you can always return it.

MIND YOUR BELONGINGS

ID: 96

I always take the bus home from the office. One time, I was seated at the second to the end row of the bus with a lady stranger. She was in her late 60's so I really didn't pay any attention to her because she seemed to be engrossed with the book that she was reading. I was also busy texting with my cell phone at that time. There was one moment during the trip that I saw something on the floor. I think it was a pen, perhaps left by a previous passenger. It was good-looking at the first glance. Because I was curious, I bent down and tried to pick it up however it rolled further under my seat so I put my bag behind me to suitably reach the thing. Abruptly, the bus stopped and some of the passengers got off. When I looked at the thing that I picked up, it was just a hard straw with different colors so I immediately put it away. I then took my bag to my lap and looked for my mobile phone. To my dismay, I couldn't find it anymore from where I had placed it, which was on the very top before I zipped the bag. What I found was my bag was already unzipped and that my wallet was missing too. I asked the other passengers if they had seen anyone who might have come to my seat and took anything. But no one could give me an answer since I was at the very end row and no one had seen anything. My suspicion was that the woman who was sitting beside me took the phone and my wallet. It just happened in an instant and I didn't even leave my bag too far from me. It was just behind my back, still on my seat. The woman didn't even look like she was capable of doing such a thing. From that day on, I make sure not to sit at the end rows of the bus as much as possible and to always be cautious of my seatmates. I always mind my belongings now and make sure not to lose sight of my things, not even for a minute.

My Lan T. Tran

WHAT YOU WEAR IS NOT WHAT YOU GET

ID: 455

When I was younger I used to lack a better judgment of people. I had met a person once who had such weird taste in terms of his clothing. He had lots of piercings on his face and had tattoos all over his arms. Although I never spoke to him directly, he always had an air of mystery so I tried to stay away from him each time I crossed his path. One day, I was getting ready to go home from school and I saw him from far away. I think he also spotted me so he started to approach. I tried to hold back my fears and picked up my pace, walking a bit more quickly. Suddenly he caught up to me and uttered a very soft greeting. I never heard him speak before so it was quite a surprise to recognize the gentleness in his voice, which was the complete opposite of how he looked on the outside. I stopped walking since he had a sense of urgency in telling me he would stop going to school because his girlfriend had just broken up with him which felt to him like it was the end of the world. He said to me he tried dangerous stuff and committing suicide to ease the pain of betrayal. In the spirit of kindness, I strongly encouraged him to walk back with me to school. We both sat down on a bench and talked about his problem a little bit more thoroughly. Instantly, I became his counselor. Years later, my little sister worked at a company and she was approached by the same person I had spoken to. He recognized the familiar last name which my sister and I shared and he asked her for my email address. I received a long note from him telling me about his life and his new family. He said in the email he could never thank me enough for that time he and I spoke even though I barely knew him. In the same email he attached a photo of himself and he was carrying his cute little daughter. I learned that appearances do not make a person at all. Everyone is fighting a hard battle one way or another. When we tune into their genuine persona, we will discover there is more we can find in their heart than the way they dress, wear their hair, or accessorize themselves.

Mistakes In Life: The Path To Wisdom

BE CAREFUL WHEN ENTERING SOMEONE'S PREMISES

ID: 270

I was invited to a new friend's house with a cousin once and had an unforgettable experience. My cousin, known to be an explorer, was more excited than I to get to the area. We hadn't gone to that house before and had only a description of the place, so I was a bit skeptical in going there however my cousin assured me that it was going to be fun being invited to a new house. So then I went along with her. When we got to the place, we were amazed by its lavish look from the outside. It had a white iron fence decorated with green archers at the top in which the arrows are pointing upwards. My cousin, as excited as I, entered the unlocked gate without using the buzzer. And so I walked after her, however when we were about to enter the main door, we were surprised by two barking, medium-sized, knee-level Doberman dogs. I was scared to death when they started to charge at us and had run back out to the gate. I saw my cousin running after me, because the dogs were as surprised as us, they went on and chase after us. Luckily, we were able to close the gate behind us and were rescued by my friend's father who heard the barking. He needed to keep the dogs to one of their rooms just to allure us to stay and enter the house. After that incident, I made sure to keep off from someone's property without asking them to accompany me when entering the premises. I made sure to beware of the neighbor's dogs too.

STEALING

ID: 34

Water flowing from a tap was unknown to me when I was a young girl, and so as far as I knew water existed only in the river. We grew up fetching water from the river every other day and this was an adventure to my friends and I. On the way to the river, there was a garden that belonged to an old man, which had a bunch of fruit. We would sneak in and steal some fruit all the time. We would delegate one kid to climb the tree and pick fruit while the rest of us collected them. One day it was my turn. I climbed the tree as usual and when I got to the top, the old man appeared and said he had finally caught the thief who had been stealing his fruit. He asked me to climb down which I did and he was ready to receive me and gave me a beating of a lifetime. He also took me to my parents and I was given another beating. From that day on I didn't dare to steal anything from anyone.

OF POOP AND PHILOSOPHY

ID: 319

My teacher always had a knack in making the discussions of our otherwise boring philosophy lessons into excursions of the weird and wonderful. On this particular day, seeing the class in a distracted mood, he suddenly asked me a question. He asked a rather ridiculous question. "Arki, have you ever seen what a cow's manure looks like?" I answered innocently, "Why, it looks like a flattened cake Sir." My teacher pressed on, "And a dog's poop?" "Hmm… It really depends, but it's usually elongated…" was my thoughtful reply. "And how about a goat's?" countered my teacher. At this I replied, "That's an easy one, everyone knows those things look like a clump of grapes." At this point, the rest of my classmates were getting nasty. And I thought, what is all these poop questions about? But my teacher did not stop there, "Now Arki, it seems like you really are knowledgeable about such things, can you tell me what a lizard's poop looks like?" I replied, "Well, that one is rather obvious, it's small and black but it has a small whitish point to it." Half the class was already chuckling at this exchange. I was unsure how this could possibly lead us into our topic. My teacher then stood and lightly patted me on my back, "Well done Arki. Now can you please tell the class, what is the name of Socrates' wife?" This caught me off-guard, and I faltered at answering the question. "So Arki…" continued my teacher, "you were not able to tell us the name of Socrates's wife, but you sure proved to us how much time you spend thinking about poop!" At this the class broke out in laughter. Lesson: Read your subject's notes in advance. This could very well save you the embarrassment I had to go through.

Mistakes In Life: The Path To Wisdom

MIND YOUR OWN BUSINESS

ID: 115

Have you ever been in the situation where people keep on asking you personal stuff that they think is just OK? Let me share with you one story where I've also had a share of these awkward moments.

It's been a habit of people to ask newly married couples: When are you having a baby? Are you having a baby yet? Are you on the way? How come you are aren't pregnant yet? What is taking you so long? Blah blah blah. I've had that habit with me since my friends started getting married. I thought it was OK, especially when they just respond to you with some funny remarks. Then when it was my turn, I found the questions intrusive to my personal life... especially when, after 5 years of being married, we still don't have a baby. It did not only feel awkward being asked those questions, but it somehow felt offensive, disrespectful, and insensitive.

I've admitted this negative feeling to people I once asked the question to, and I said sorry. I told them I now know what it feels like.

Lesson learned is simple – Mind your own business.

BREAKING UP IS HARD TO DO

ID: 491

I grew up in a very conservative and traditional family, with a strict and disciplinarian father and a very lenient mother. For me my father was a real life monster, we grew up as battered children. My mother was a battered wife, yet I wondered why she never complained nor ran away with us. Despite the beatings she still served my father like her master. I do hate her for that because we saw how my father beat her.

When I was in high school I promised to myself that when I got married, I would never be like my mother. I would never bow down to any man's will. Instead, I would let my husband bow down on me. It should be my voice that must be followed. Well, to make the story short, I was married, to a man who is 17 years older than I.

As I have promised myself, I will never ever be like my mother; for that, I became a tyrant like my father. I was so domineering, possessive, so demanding and all of the negative qualities I had seen from my father were all inside me. In short, I become an entire replica of my father; I never become a battered wife, but I became a husband beater. And one more thing, I never served him ever since we got married.

Since he was a soldier; I was always left alone with our daughter. He stayed at his post for more than three months, in a year I could just count the number of days he was with us. One day he asked me to go with him to the place where he was assigned, I refused, I just stayed at home. Then, he told me to never blame him if by chance he found someone who would take care of him. Because of my PRIDE I told him to go ahead, it wouldn't be my loss.

Perhaps it was a challenge or maybe it was his way to stay away from temptation but I was too proud and over-confident that he would never find someone as pretty and as young as me. Months had passed after that, and I never heard from him anymore. I was scared that something might have happened to him on the battlefield. One day the wife of his fellow soldier asked me to go with her to the military campsite where both of our husbands were assigned; because I was worried I went with her. I was supposed to go directly to his quarter when we arrived, but my friend told me we would just surprise him at night.

Well, I agreed and even grinned imagining my husband's surprised face. It was around 10 pm when I finally knocked on his quarter's door. And to my surprise a woman holding an infant opened the door. I felt like I was a mad woman, I was in a wild frenzy at that time. If only my husband was paper, I would have torn him into a million pieces that night.

Some officers and men in the military camp brought us into their office to pacify and iron things out. I was still clawing him in my fury. First thing in the morning I went home still fuming; I told myself that I will file for annulment right then and there. After a month, he finally went home, he asked for a second chance, but I never gave it to him. I was hurt, I felt

Mistakes In Life: The Path To Wisdom

insulted and most of all I felt so sorry for myself for all the things that I had ever done to him.

Even if I wanted to take him back, my wounded pride would never allow it; in short we got separated. He gave me allotment for our daughter as I demanded, but I was never happy. That was more than two decades ago, but the pain and the hurt is still there; nonetheless, I have to keep moving forward of course with regrets in my heart because I could never find a man as good as him.

Lesson: There will always be a point in our life when we need to choose between love and PRIDE; my advice is let love lead the way, never let pride eat your whole being otherwise you will end up living the rest of your life with regrets.

MOBILE PHONE

ID: 55

Mobile phones have made it easier to tell lies because people can't tell where you actually are or whether you're doing what you say you're doing. One day a friend of mine called me, asking if I was in town so that we could meet in order for me to pay her back some cash I owed her. Because I knew I was short of cash at that time, I told her I was at home. What I didn't know was that my friend had seen me in town, and she wanted to confirm if it was me she had seen. After finishing the conversation, she walked right over to where I was. At that moment, I wished the ground would swallow me because I was so ashamed of telling a lie. I learned to tell the truth on the phone no matter what. The truth will always set you free, always say it.

My Lan T. Tran

TRUST YOUR INSTINCTS

ID: 346

I work on a lot of theater productions in my spare time. When I commit to something, they have my word that I am going to follow through. My friend Amanda called me one night, knowing that I would be someone who she could count on and asked if I would be willing to step into a show that she was working on at the last minute because someone had dropped out. I had a feeling in my gut that this was not going to go well, but after looking at my schedule I was able to be there so I told her I would help out. When I got to the first rehearsal I was attending, it was complete chaos. There were kids in the show that were running around like crazy, the director was yelling at everyone, and there was no organization at all. I was there for the next couple of weeks, learning my small part and getting more and more frustrated. By the time the show went on, I was completely fed up with how terribly disorganized these people were, and was very glad it was over. The show had been over an hour away from my house and being at rehearsal and the shows had cost me a lot of money in gas. I learned to always trust my instincts when something like this pops up. Even though I helped a friend out, I realized that they had plenty of people who were interested in the small role, and I was simply a fill in that nobody cared was being majorly inconvenienced. I will always ask more questions in the beginning from now on.

I WAS DRUNK

ID: 149

I was drunk last night and I said terrible things to my wife. I'm sure I had hurt her feelings so much that she left and went to her hometown. I just found out a while ago when I came home today from work. I tried calling her but she's not answering the phone. I feel so bad to have done it. Too much alcohol really brings out the worst of me. I can't think straight at all; everything I see are the things that went wrong in our relationship and my life. I've been in circles these past few weeks. I'm trying to let my wife know but I don't know how to express it. I have this terrible feeling inside me... a loneliness that I don't really know the cause. I know now that alcohol won't help a bit. It will only worsen things, but I still need help. How can I win her back again? How can I start telling her what's going on with me?

THE HOUSE OF OUR DREAMS

ID: 516

Our family has been renting apartments and houses. We've been wanting to have our own house where we could comfortably dwell and accept relatives and friends. We enjoy driving around villages and looking for nice houses and praying for it until I came across a house for sale on the internet. I asked my husband to take a look at the terms. The following day, we went to take a look at it. It was exactly the house I've been dreaming about. We called up the agent and discussed the terms. They even offered better terms and gave us time to prepare for the down payment.

Finally, we made it! We worked for the amount we needed and borrowed the rest from our parents. Because we were overwhelmed with excitement, we overlooked the other bills we had. But we still believed we could settle the monthly amortization, not considering that we were about to send our daughter to college the next year and that means renting a place for her while amortizing the house we purchased. During the first months, we were able to settle the amortizations. The following months, we began to struggle. There were several times our electric services were disconnected and we began having overdue balances on our other payables.

We then realized that we were struggling and it was not God's will for us to have that house. We believe that when God blesses, He adds no trouble into it. As we struggled to make payments for the house, we needed to sacrifice the car we were also paying through amortization. It was like losing so much of our hard earned money.

We began failing to fund our checks for the house amortization and started to receive notices to vacate the house. We felt bad but realized that we failed to plan. As they say, if you fail to plan, you plan to fail.

My Lan T. Tran

We ended up giving up everything. We lost our house and our car. All the money we paid was forfeited in favor of the owner of the house and the bank financing the car. I was humiliated but that's the price I had to pay for not planning properly and by being impulsive.

MISSING CHOCOLATE

ID: 73

I think most people on this website love to eat chocolate, like me. I LOVE to eat white chocolate. My mom would buy a bag of these small white chocolate balls, and every time I was good she would give me one. One day she wasn't looking so I took a hand full of them and just sat there eating them. I wasn't too clever on where to hide the wrappers so I just hid them under her bed sheets. Little did I know that that was the same day she was changing the sheets. She found about 7 chocolate wrappers, and she immediately knew that I was the one who had done it, but she made me admit it first. She questioned me about it and I ended up lying to her. Well, I ended up getting busted, and she stopped buying the chocolate balls. Lesson learned, if you did something wrong and someone questions you about it, you might as well just tell the truth.

PREVENTION IS ALWAYS BETTER THAN CURE

ID: 379

Yes, we've all heard this cliché before. However, I bet few people realize the truth in this. The fact is, rather than thinking much about future consequences, we tend to revel only in the here and the now.

I work at a construction site. For those who may not be familiar with the culture bred in such a workplace, there are only two things that make all the people come together: Food and alcohol! On regular occasions, we would gather and prepare lots of food and drinks as if a government official would visit us. These celebrations were always so happy that during those nights, all the site's problems are momentarily forgotten. For us engineers, it was also an opportunity to bond with sub-contractors and supervisors so that despite the occasional spats, we were able to gain their trust and loyalty back. We didn't even care if the next day, some people would be absent nursing hangovers. Unfortunately, certain things come with a price.

Our company requires all employees to get physical check-ups at least once every year. A month after I had lab tests done, the company doctor called me asking me to report to the main office. There, he showed me the results and discussed what was wrong. My liver enzymes were so high that he was wondering why I wasn't showing signs of jaundice yet. He had other procedures done on me that confirmed I had Grade 3 fatty liver which was serious as conditions like this could lead to problems such as cirrhosis or liver cancer. He warned me that I had no other choice but to take certain medications and more importantly, to drastically change my lifestyle and diet so that further damage could be prevented. He was even doubtful at first as to how far I could recover since little was expected for cases like mine. Luckily, after a few months, I managed to lessen the gravity of my disease from Grade 3 to Grade 1 with exercise and a lot of self-discipline.

As the Dalai Lama said when asked about what surprised him most about humanity, "Man. Because he sacrifices his health in order to make money. Then he sacrifices money to recuperate his health. And then he is so anxious about the future that he does not enjoy the present; the result being that he does not live in the present or the future; he lives as if he is never going to die, and then dies having never really lived."

JUST DON'T ANSWER

ID: 186

Everyone has a story of how they were embarrassed by a parent or relative. Well I was embarrassed by my horseback riding instructor. She did not mean to embarrass me, nor did I mean to make it worse by answering. You could say it was 50-50. We were at a horse show with our little ragtag group of competitors. We had someone showing in almost every class. At a horse show there are different classes for different horse types in which they must do different activities. Each horse and rider has a number that is assigned at the beginning of the show. You are awarded prizes when the judge calls your number and places you, normally first through sixth place. It is imperative that a rider knows their number. When you decide you do not want to ride in a class but have already been registered you go to the registration booth and scratch from that class. The term scratch is what got me into trouble. I was across the rather large arena having a soda when my number was called over the loud speaker to enter the class. It was an error and I was not in the class, but my trainer also recognized my number. She was on the opposite end of the arena from me and suddenly I hear, "Amanda, go scratch yourself, this isn't your class." Everyone was looking around to see who the recipient of this comment was since it sounded so off key. Stupidly, I answered her saying nothing but "I don't need to scratch myself someone else has taken care of it." I instantly realized what had been said in the exchange and turned bright red. My lesson learned that day was to think before you speak, or at least before you yell an answer across a crowded park.

IF I WAS A LITTLE MORE CAREFUL!
ID: 554

At my 19th birthday, my mother gave me a new cellphone, and it was a Nokia-N9. I liked it very much, actually I was waiting for a gift like that. I was so grateful to my mother for the gift. But, alas! I could not use the cellphone more than 2 months. One night it was stolen from my bed. That night, I was sleeping by the window and the cell was very close to the window. The thief had taken it easily while I was sleeping. As thievery is a problem in our town & is common, I am always careful about small and valuable things. But that night, I was really careless. After waking at morning, I told myself, "the thief didn't take it, I gave it away". I said this because the thief got the opportunity because of me. If I was a little more careful, I wouldn't have lost the gift.

Mistakes In Life: The Path To Wisdom

NICE TO HAVE SEVERAL BAGS, BUT...

ID: 226

... make sure you keep your things in tact!

As you may already have guessed, I have several bags that I swap with each other several times during the week. I use a bag organizer so that I make sure that I have everything I need, no matter what my bag is. This wasn't true for me two years ago.

I always make it a point to match my bag to my attire, yet I don't really prepare my stuff ahead of time. Which meant... I had to leave for work in 10 minutes, yet I was still transferring my stuff from one bag to the other. This laziness (as I would call it) hit me big time when I forgot to put my debit card in my new bag. It was Thursday, my shopping day. As I was about to pay, heat rushed to my face when I remembered that I actually forgot to take my debit card with me. Worse, I had some bundle of cash in the pocket of my other bag, I could have used that too! I was so embarrassed, I was even in the exclusive shoppers' lane when this happened. I just acted surprised and worried that someone took my purse. I don't remember people's reactions but I rushed outside.

I immediately bought myself a bag organizer the following weekend now I make it a point to use that everyday. Never failed me so far.

LIFE IS SHORT

ID: 409

When I was in high school, I always went out with my friends and never cared or visited my dying grandmother. I thought that what I had done was the right thing because I never expected that she would die. I was so guilty because I never even tried to say thank you to my grandmother when she was still alive. Life is really too short, we really need to say what we should want to say to our love ones before it's too late. Don't wait for the right time because that right time might not come in your life.

My Lan T. Tran

STICK TO YOUR PLAN

ID: 574

When I was a freshman student, the university where I was studying was hundreds of kilometers away from my home. I hadn't gone before to that city where the university was located. My family sent money per month for educational stuff. Since I had no experience saving money, I spent all that I had on unnecessary things. I went to restaurants and ate expensive food and drinks; I enjoyed spending money for parties, gambling and so on. Before the end of each month, I lost all the money so I asked my family to send extra money. I remember my father advised me on the phone. He said, "Son, a long run of life is awaiting you that you must struggle with and be a winner, otherwise all you have imagined will be full of weeds with no results, think wisely." Then, I openly told to my father the void stuffs that I had experienced. He cried and forgave what I had done in the university; I also cried from my heart and since that time on I changed my ways by strictly concentrating on my education and removing my bad characters and the money was more than enough.

CHEATING

ID: 10

My sophomore English teacher in high school was awful. She was not a role model, from the way she taught to the way she dressed. None of us respected her. She would fall asleep almost every Friday when we had vocabulary quizzes or tests. A bunch of kids cheated. I did too, which meant I didn't learn much English that year. At the time, I thought I was lucky to have such an easy teacher, but now that I've grown up, I realize that I was unfortunate. I didn't cheat the school system, I cheated myself and robbed myself of the knowledge I could have obtained. The best teachers were the ones that gave me so much work that I had wished they would die every day in class, lol. Those were the ones that actually cared about us kids and wanted us to do better in life.

Cheating in school was the first mistake. The second mistake was using someone else as an excuse to take the easy route out. Life is short when

Mistakes In Life: The Path To Wisdom

it's fun and good, but it can be a long and miserable journey if you take the wrong path. Always invest in yourself and love yourself regardless whether or not the world, including your family, believes in you or cares about you. You are the best and last allied force you can have in your life.

BLEACH STAINS

ID: 98

My first major mistake in life occurred when I was about nine years old. I am sure I had many before then, but this mistake earned me a spanking from my grandmother. Until that time I did not know that grandmas could punish people. They were only there to treat and pamper and offer ice cream after dinner. That fateful weekday afternoon I learned that grandmas could spank, even when you had the best intentions. I had been drinking red Kool Aid in the living room which I was not supposed to do, but Grandma never seemed to mind. At least Grandma never minded until that day. I tIpped over my glass and spilled red Kool Aid all over Grandma's light tan carpet. I immediately panicked and grabbed a towel to sop up the spreading mess. The towel did little to remove the ever growing red stain. I remember thinking of how mom got red juice out of my favorite white shirt. She soaked it in bleach and then rinsed it with water. I knew where grandma kept her bleach so I ran for the laundry room. I poured a full cup of bleach and soaked a towel with water. I took the bleach and carefully poured it over the huge red stain. The smell was overwhelming, but I persevered and wet down the bleach with the towel and was happy to see that the red was gone. Then I started to get worried, because not only was the red gone, but so was the color from the carpet. I didn't know what to do so I did what any scared nine year old would do, I sat on the spot and pretended it didn't happen. When Grandma walked in she immediately smelled the bleach. I looked up nervously and she made me get up. My soaked jeans now also had a bright white spot from all the bleach. Grandma freaked out to say the least. She yelled and lectured and ultimately spanked. I tried to tell her I was just cleaning like she taught me, but to no avail. I learned an important lesson that day, I learned bleach is not just for removing stains, it also leaves them. This was a lesson that for years I was reminded of as grandma always had one oddly placed rug in her living room, at least until she replaced the carpet.

TO LOVE AND BE LOVED
ID: 457

I started smoking at the age of 15, and started being an alcoholic at the age of 16. I was so addicted back then, with all the parties I kept attending. I always had money that I could waste on drinks or girls. Life was a big party.

I entered college and immediately found myself lots of friends. Being in college, I always thought that I needed to be like everybody else. I got more addicted to my vices and started failing all my grades. For years, I was trapped in a life where I couldn't seem to escape. I got tired; it was always a cycle, getting wasted every day, getting scolded by my parent, or being dumped by a girlfriend. I craved for help, and I wanted to change.

Luckily, I was saved by my friends from home. They lifted me up from the struggles I went through. I started attending seminars, listening to people sharing who had been like me. I also met the girl I was longing for, someone who understands, someone whom I don't have to pretend to be someone else for, just me. Love saved me, love from my family, friends, and from my special someone. Indeed, it is so wonderful to love, and to be loved.

DON'T PUSH IT WHEN YOU ARE SICK
ID: 272

I am one of those bizarre people who enjoys exercising. I go to the gym despite injury or illness. I always go when I have a cold. This may have been okay in my 20's but it's not working for me in my 30's. I pushed myself to my limits a few months ago when my cold turned into a persistent cough that eventually needed medical attention. Turned out that my exercise

Mistakes In Life: The Path To Wisdom

routine had forced the infection to spread and I ended up with bronchitis. Next time, I will take a couple of days off from the gym.

VOUS PARLEZ LE 'BLEEP'?

ID: 36

Those were exactly the words (except for bleep which actually represents vulgarity) I spoke to a female course mate who is very fluent in French since she lived in Togo most of her life. I was in my second year at the university. A rebel, living for the moment and no thought about my actions. Now we had to choose an elective course for the semester. I chose French (cringe) because it didn't only appear to be a playful class but there was this mademoiselle who caught my fancy with her French like gait.

I didn't even know how to introduce my self in French so I stuck at the back of the class and reduced my average height (sitting) to avoid getting spotted by the lecturer during question time. For me, it was fun. I could get away with it. The only thing I needed was Mademoiselle's private classes.

On judgment day it dawned on me that I knew nothing French except the word mademoiselle (and a few others that I didn't care to use). I approached her (my romantic interest) and told her my problem. She said she would assist me and it seemed that all my prayers had been answered. Unfortunately, the invigilator was le diable (the devil) himself. I got accustomed to the word on meeting this man who relished the idea of getting any unfortunate student to sign the exam malpractice form. You should have seen the way he was all over me. He kept screaming in his high pitched voice asking me to sit up straight, place my hands where he could see them, look at the paper, stop looking left, right or turning back, etc. While he was screaming at me, I could see other students sneaking papers to each other.

Like it wasn't bad enough, the guy relocated me to the wilderness (no one on the left, right or behind me). It made me sweat. Mademoiselle was like three rows away and I needed her to help me out because I could not imagine myself coming back to rewrite the exam next year (which I eventually did).

The invigilator's (le diable) phone rang and he went out to take the very private call. I saw this as my chance and took off for mademoiselle's slightly outstretched hands that contained the solution to my problem (a complete answer script). But, talk about le diable, the next thing I heard was "stay like that. Just stay like that" he was chuckling as he approached.

I abandoned the answer script and walked back to my seat. He began to shout that he asked me to remain where I was. But I needed to get hold of my papers on the desk or he would use it against me later. With this (my registration number) in hand I ran to the door but he followed. My course mates roared as we both struggled at the door. But I managed to escape and jumped from the corridor to the gravel below (about 8 feet).

I had regrets. I sustained some cuts from that stunt. I had to rewrite the course the following year. But I was quick to learn my lessons which I am grateful for. I have learned that we should do the right things for the right reasons. Studying French just to get close to someone was not ideal. Whenever you have the chance to make a difference use it well. The fact that you "think" you are not good enough in one or more subjects does not determine your destiny. All that is required from you is work and faith. Only you can make a true statement about yourself, no body else can. You have to make a statement and live up to it. Work and faith my friends. It is never too late to make changes in our lives.

DON'T PICK!

ID: 320

Time for a gross story. We all know that we aren't supposed to pick at things like pimples and sores but many of us do anyway. When I was 16 I had a rather late in life severe case of the chicken pox. I got a giant sore on my chin that I couldn't resist picking. 16 years later, I still have a big scar on my face as a reminder to leave my skin blemishes alone.

Mistakes In Life: The Path To Wisdom

DOUBLE-CHECK HUNDRED TIMES

ID: 116

When shopping once, I failed to double-check the actual price of the item I brought to the counter. The store was having a sale and offering up to 50% discounts on most of their stuff. I picked up a shirt from the rack that had a red tag posted on it saying all the items displayed were 50% off. I thought that it was a good deal because I only had to pay $15.00 for that signature shirt instead of paying the usual regular price. I was on a tight budget as well, so buying an extra shirt was a luxury at that moment. Yet, I still decided to go for that discounted price because I couldn't shake off the fact that I'd be paying half the price for a signature shirt that I really liked. I went to the counter excitedly and patiently waited on the very long queue, just to get my adored shirt. When it was my turn to be served, the sales lady punched the item on the cash register and to my surprise, the amount was $30.00. I told her that it was from the 50% off shelf, conformingly she said that the price of $30.00 was already a discounted price from the actual amount of $60.00. Seeing that the people after me were already staring and impatient of the fuss going on and that I was already mortified, I had then decided resentfully to just pay for the item to end that embarrassing situation. At the end, I regretfully spent a very much needed amount of money to an overpriced shirt that I really didn't need at that moment.

I really learned something that day – a lesson to be always attentive and be careful of every detail. Always double-check before you decide on things.

SAVING FOR THE RAINY DAYS

ID: 486

There was a point in my life when my husband and I were earning more than what we needed; because we started from rags, we were so overwhelmed when a huge amount of money came in. Because of that, we always had more than our fair share of shopping, dining out and worse we learned to gamble. Every night we were always there at the casino. We never cared how much money we lost at the slot machines because the blessings continuously came in.

My Lan T. Tran

There was never a day that we missed going to the casino. We never realized that, it was also the very reason we lost everything. Both of us were addicted to it especially when my husband won not just by hundreds but by thousands in our currency. However, that was not for long because one day my husband lost his appetite and drastically lost weight. I was more alarmed when he had a fever and his eyes started to turn yellowish. I brought him to the hospital and to my dismay; he was diagnosed of having Hepatitis B, worse of all he had to be confined right away. I was unprepared for that, the doctor told us to prepare a hefty sum for my husband to get well.

Because we didn't have any savings, and just a bit more money left, I began to worry as to where to get the money needed for his hospitalization. The things I did to raise money.... I sold all of my jewelry and our first car. It was so painful to let go all of those material things; however, I needed to save the life of my husband. With the proceeds of what I sold I paid all of the hospital bills and there was still enough money for his medication.

When he was discharged from the hospital and we were on our way home; none of us spoke. Each of us were in deep thought, contemplating on what had happened and what would happen next. When we arrived at home, he finally spoke. He told me that he was sorry he got sick. I told him it was not his fault since everyone of us could get sick. The fault we had was that we never cared to save. If only we had just saved the money we wasted in the casino; perhaps my jewelry would still be with me and most especially our car.

Because of that incident we learned our lesson well. From that time on, we never went to the casino anymore. When my husband was well enough and went back to work, we agreed to save extra money not only for rainy days, but also for our son's education. By God's grace we have moved on, and with our savings we bought another car and sent our son to a private school. The formula we used for our success is this, Income – Savings = Expenses.

Lesson: We must never indulge in gambling, it will just bring us down; instead of spending our money on nothing, it's better for us to save it to prepare us for the time we need it most.

Mistakes In Life: The Path To Wisdom

OVER NIGHT TRAVELING

ID: 56

During my campus life, I had a habit of traveling at night even when I had time during the day. I continued this habit for a long time. Then one day I took a night bus to a rural area. Unfortunately, it was not my lucky day because in the middle of nowhere, the bus developed a mechanical problem. We were forced to spend the night in the cold because the problem could only be fixed in the morning. It was in a forest and there were wild animals roaming around. We were all terrified and we weren't sure if we would make it till morning. Thankfully, we made it! The bus was repaired and we continued driving. I learned my lesson, and now I only travel at night when I can't avoid it. My advice is that if you're driving, don't do it at night if you are all alone and you are passing through unsafe places. Or at least make sure the vehicle you're using won't break down.

DO A BUDGET BEFORE MAKING LIFE-CHANGING PURCHASES

ID: 347

We bought our first home 2 years ago. I had a nagging suspicion that it was beyond our means but I gave in and signed as a guarantor on the mortgage. Right after we moved in, I got accepted into a prestigious legal program that was going to cost over $20,000. It was a full-time course load too. Instead of being able to quit my job and focus on my studies, I had to work full-time and go to school full-time because we are basically "house poor". We haven't missed any mortgage payments, but I can guarantee that my health suffered due to all of the stress that I have endured over the past 2 years while burning the candle at both ends. Listen to your gut. Make sure that you have enough to pay for your home should one of you lose your job.

My Lan T. Tran

TURN OFF THE MICROPHONE
ID: 153

When I taught students in a special needs classroom, I was asked to wear an auditory trainer. If you are not familiar with this device it is actually very cool. Students with hearing difficulties are given a headset and the classroom is equipped with speakers so that the teacher can be heard with clarity even for those with hearing difficulties. The teacher has a small headset and a battery pack that is wirelessly connected to the other components. I got very used to wearing the gadget and it truly was helpful to the students who were hard of hearing. Well as teachers often do, I took advantage of a free moment to run to the restroom while another teacher was watching my classroom. I had just sat down to pee when I heard frantic knocking at the door and a burst of laughter. I finished up and as I was adjusting my skirt I felt the battery pack and suddenly realized my major mistake. I forgot rule number one of having an auditory trainer, always turn it off in the restroom. My entire class of youngsters had heard me relieving myself. I learned a very embarrassing lesson that day that I have yet to live down.

BACK IN MY HIGH SCHOOL
ID: 517

Back in my high school, I really made lots of mistakes. The story goes like this, every first Friday of the month there was a survey for the teachers, and they were evaluated on the way they teach their students. There was a supervisor, the school principal, and some respected teachers. Then our teacher gave an activity. We were given a piece of paper and there was a word on it which corresponded to the correct answer of the question that our teacher asked. I felt so nervous; all I was thinking was that I needed to put the answer on the board. While our teacher was talking, I stood up and got in front of the board and I put the piece of paper there, then I felt that everyone in the classroom was staring at me, my classmates were about to laugh. That was the time that I realized that my teacher did not ask a question yet. I was so embarrass at that moment, I wanted to disappear, and I wanted to hide! All I could do was to keep quiet and pretend that nothing happened. Sometimes when I remember that moment, I just tell myself it is just part of life, everyone makes mistakes, and the important thing is that I learned from my mistakes. What I have learned from this experience is that I should not be so nervous that I lose my focus and avoid doing some foolish things.

JUMPING THE QUEUE

ID: 74

Recently I went to the bank and saw that there was a very long line, so I decided to by-pass others. No one bothered to question me so I thought I would be served quickly without wasting my time. When I got to the counter, the cashier denied me service because she had seen what I had done. I got very mad but no one bothered to listen to me. All the other customers laughed at me, I felt very embarrassed and I walked away from the bank. Deep in my heart, I knew I was wrong but I couldn't stand the eyes that were looking at me anymore. The next time you want to by-pass others, think twice because you don't know who is looking at you. I learned to respect others and also to be patient because everyone is in a hurry and it is first come first served.

PATIENCE IS A VIRTUE

ID: 381

When I first started college I was very poor. I had a car, but it was a junker, falling apart at the seams. Worst of all it had no heat, and I lived in Western New York. It gets very very cold here. One night I got into my car and the windshield was all frosted over. I decided that I didn't want to wait, and I was only going a couple blocks, so I cleared a small section and started moving. I ended up hitting a sign in the parking lot that I had been parked in, and needed my friends to come and get me. I was very upset and worried about how I was going to pay for the damage. That was a very difficult time for me, but it taught me a valuable lesson about patience. I knew that my windshield was not going to clear on its own, so I needed to take the time to scrape it off before moving.

HE HAS GIVEN ME NEW HOPE

ID: 192

You could say that I am a very patient and enduring person. I was born to an average income type of family and every penny you spent, you needed to earn it first. After college, I made it a point to find a job immediately to help my parents support the education of my two younger brothers. I worked various kinds of jobs, even if I was underemployed and underpaid. I guess this is what you mostly get during these days, unless you already have the money or business to run on your own or know a lot of people and got the job that you wanted but I didn't. So, I really tried very hard to stay on my hard-earned meager paying job just to earn money and help my family. I had lots of sacrifices, like going to another city, which was very far from my hometown and lived alone, without any relatives or friends that I could run to for any emergency cases, advice or emotional support. I also experienced not eating enough just to allocate most of my pay to my brothers' education funds. All of this, because I believe that they too deserve to reach their dreams and I knew that they would someday share in helping my poor parents. However, one particular piece of news from home had devastated me and I felt that I was betrayed. My parents told me that my other brother who was in second year college got a girl pregnant and decided to stop schooling all at once and just marry his girlfriend. The girl was also in college like him with no job and was quite young to start a family. I cried several days upon hearing the news and had somehow lost a piece of my future.

I felt so angry with my brother and had called him on the phone. I said several harsh and hurtful words including how I gave up my self-happiness and made a lot of sacrifices just to support his education. I enumerated all the things that I provided him. He in return, said things that hurt me more, like he had not asked for me to do these things for him and all. I was not only angry with him at that time but also with my parents who let those things happen. It made me a bitter person full of sadness and hopelessness in my heart.

I only got back to being myself again when my younger brother showed me that he could finish his education and be successful. He changed the way I look at situations now; he said that he had known of me and my parents' sacrifices and that he didn't want to disappoint us again. He had witnessed my brother's struggling family life and he didn't want to go through the situation again. He is now a professional and successful person and the one primarily supporting our aging parents. He has given me new hope. It only takes one inspiration to go on living your dreams again.

I promise not to lose hope ever again.

PLEASE TRY TO CONTROL YOUR ANGER

ID: 556

It was January 1st, 2012, the beginning of a new year. And it was also the day of the annual feast of our hall (Amar Ekusey Hall), one of the student halls of our varsity. That day a terrible incident happened there. Because of a misunderstanding between two political student groups, a quarrel took place and turned into fighting. That fight caused ten students to become seriously injured. I was with one of the groups and I am kind of a leader of that group. Because of that fight, 21 students were suspended from varsity for one year and I was one of them.

Now I am banished from my campus, my friends and also from my academic carrier. Now I realize what a great mistake I made then. I could have stopped that fight, had I tried. If I hadn't gotten angry, if I had controlled my anger, I could have stayed at my varsity, been with my friends and continued my studies without any break.

My Lan T. Tran

IT'S NOT WORTH THE HUMILIATION

ID: 230

I remember back in high school when I was too lazy to study. I always went to class late and unprepared. There was an instance when I was absent for three consecutive days and had no idea of the current lessons of the class. As expected I was not prepared for one of my professor's weekly exams. As always, I asked my closest friend and seatmate to let me take a peek of her paper for answers. I was able to pull off this act often since my professor didn't really care about checking the class during test sessions. He just sat on his desk or sometimes would go out for a quick break. So, I did the copying too well again and was confident that I had passed the exam. Or so I thought. When the results came, most of my classmates' papers were returned and were announced to have passed, including my closest classmate. However, mine was not called and so I wondered what had happened for the rest of the class hour. When the class ended, my professor asked me to stay for a while because we needed to talk. I had the strongest feeling it was about my exam paper. Maybe I failed the test or maybe I was busted.

I was nervous and it got worst when my teacher started the conversation by asking "Did you study before the exam?" "How did you come to know the subject to be tested?" I didn't know how to answer him and was able to come up with the alibi that I borrowed my classmate's notes the day before and reviewed it. His eyebrows narrowed and very firmly said that he hated people who didn't tell the truth and cheated. I could feel my sweat coming out and heartbeat pounding hard. He further said that one of my answers had my classmates name on it. He showed it to me and unfortunately....it was true that I had written my classmate's name on the essay letter draft test section. I overlooked the fill in the blank part and automatically wrote someone's name instead of mine. No words came out after I saw the paper and my teacher told me to go to the principal's office. The incident had reached my parents and I was grounded for several weeks. The news had also spread to my classmates and the humiliation made me realize that it was not worth the bad deed. That incident made me study more instead of copying answers from my classmate. It made me a good student and a better person. I learned the bad side of cheating. I learned to value honesty sincerely since then.

Mistakes In Life: The Path To Wisdom

DEPENDENCE ON ALCOHOL

ID: 412

Everyone has different ways of coping up with their problems. Some share it with other people, while others only wait for the solution to come. Mostly, people get themselves drunk, and I was one of them.

I got so dependent and addicted to alcohol that in every minor problem, I would get drunk. Failed an exam? After school hours, I would get myself a drink or two. Dumped by a girl? I got myself two more drinks. My life revolved around it so much that I always tried to forget by engulfing myself in alcohol. One by one, friends left me, as well as my girlfriend. My family also had enough of me that they didn't care anymore about me. I felt so alone, and useless. Until one day, I found myself swimming in my own pool of puke. I was so ashamed of myself, and imagined how pitiful I looked like. I wondered if I still could change.

Slowly, I recovered. I became more open and talked to my friends all the time. I felt so light-hearted, and I wondered why I never tried doing this before. I realized that people who care are always around you, just waiting for you to reach out. From then on, I won over alcohol.

6TH SENSE

ID: 576

Meeting people and sharing always brings joy to me in ways I can't explain. I meet my friends often with intentions of learning something new or just being supportive depending on the situation. As time goes on, you realize you can easily sniff out people's intentions with you, if they are genuine or just want to have fun or they are serious with you.

I was not dating when I met this guy I shall call Peter. He was introduced to me by a guy I had a huge crush on and he clearly was not interested as he set me up with his best friend. From that moment I knew something was amiss and I held my tongue not to cause a scene. Peter took an interest right from the start and I was polite enough to accept meeting up with him as I thought he was just good company. I struggled with judging him but my gut kept insisting that I should not trust him. After 2 months of seeing each other randomly-I noticed a pattern that raised my eyebrows with suspicion.

Peter had an addiction with alcohol but he denied it over and over saying that it was just to get his energy up. The situation got worse and he had tequila shots every 3 hours and he started lying to my face and the cycle kept on and on. I slowed down on meeting him but he kept at it, making it up to me by doing things that I liked. His intentions were good but he was obviously a wreck.

The last straw on the camel's back was when I made a trip out of town and he never showed up and worst of all he got into a club fight after a guy hit on me and he claimed to be defending my honor as he was my boyfriend. He was claiming me as property and that did not make me feel good at all.

It took a lot of guts but I had a straight talk with him and I had to dump him-and I was not even dating him-and I had to cut all ties with him including his best friend who had set me up with him in the first place. Had I listened to my gut from the first day, I would have not gone through so much drama. It was a lesson I learned heavily-listen to your gut and take precaution.

KARMA'S A FISH

ID: 12

One night my aunt, my sisters, and I sat in a bedroom trying to remember all the silly, funny, and stupid mistakes we made in life. I told the fish story (ID #5) and we all laughed UNTIL suddenly my aunt's laughter was cut short. Her eyes rolled up as if she remembered something from the past. Then she gave me a death stare and said "Grandma never owned any fish! THAT was MY fish!!! I never knew how it died!!" Next time before I tell any story of any pet I accidentally killed, I will make sure to verify the owner of that pet with the crowd first.

Mistakes In Life: The Path To Wisdom

SAVE FOR THE STORM

ID: 99

Before, I considered myself as a one day millionaire. When I have money, it does not take long before I spend it all. Every payday, I can't wait to go shopping or go out with friends. I bought mostly things that I didn't really need like another pair of shoes or new set of jeans and different sorts of accessories. Those were things that I already have which were still quite new and usable. I didn't really care if the only money I had left was the budget for food and transportation. I didn't think of saving for the future. I always thought that I would always have funds because I had a job. Not until the recession affected the company I was working with. Most of the employees were sent on forced leave. I was one of those who was put on leave without pay. The hardest part was I had no funds to support myself during those weeks when I was out of a job. Fortunately, I had families and friends who extended their help. But that event has taught me a lesson of the importance of preparing for the future. It also made me realize the significance of living below your means so you can save for unavoidable crises in your life. I always make sure now to put aside a portion of my salary as my savings. No matter how little the value I save each time, I'm still at peace that I will have something to fall back on when the worst times come.

PREPARING YOUR STUFF FOR WORK THE NIGHT BEFORE

ID: 459

As a teacher, I should always be prepared and set up my materials for tomorrow's lessons. When I was just starting out in the profession many years ago, I had a really bad habit of leaving everything to the last minute. My friends would tell me to prepare my stuff the night before so that I would not miss anything the following day, but I never listened.

One day I had a very important presentation to make and out of stress, I completely forgot everything that I needed to do, including the things I should have rehearsed. Instead, I went out to do other things which were unimportant. My friends invited me to go see a movie and even though I knew I was going to have a class the following morning, I still went out with them. I enjoyed this a lot and even stayed up late because I did not want to miss all the fun my friends were having. When it was time to go to bed, I dismissed the idea that I should prepare my stuff. When I woke up, I barely had 15 minutes to prepare myself which I did not expect since I had planned to wake up an hour earlier. I crammed, panicked, and lost control of my emotions. It was totally embarrassing when I went to school and had a very poor performance in one of my classes and felt really guilty about delivering something I did not manage to organize well. When I got home, I had never felt so much remorse that I talked myself into changing my behavior.

I must be ready all the time; as a teacher, I have the moral responsibility towards my students and at the same time, the conscience that I must deliver the best lessons there are and never settle for less. More than the embarrassment, I also felt that if I want to get the respect from students and colleagues, I should become more organized, responsible, and prepared all the time when it comes to my materials and lessons.

IT TAKES A LITTLE COURAGE

ID: 275

Growing up as a very shy girl, I had no confidence in expressing myself especially to an audience. My mother encouraged me to join in sports particularly in track and field when I was in school, in order that I become trained in the values of sportsmanship, one of which is the courage to accept the fact, as in real life, that only the person who did their best would take home the medal and the rest of us could do better the next time. I think this is one of the greatest lessons I have carried through into my adulthood. Once I sent out more than a dozen job applications and did not receive any response from any one of them, and in effect, it made me feel everything I have done in life was a complete failure. Instead of thinking about all the rejections, I tried changing my perspective by remembering

Mistakes In Life: The Path To Wisdom

the lessons learned from each and every track and field event which I either won or lost.

Losing is not the end of everything – it takes more courage to get back up again and continue running than to sink deeper into regret and feel depressed about it as this would only make you miss out on better opportunities that come your way.

LYING TO MISS SCHOOL
ID: 37

I know that when we all start school it's fun for a little while, but then it becomes such a bother that we all wish school had never started. This is very common with many children and I was not an exception. When the weather was cold and I felt like I needed some more sleep, I would complain to my mother that I was sick and I couldn't attend school. She would eventually give in to my complaints, but she would insist that I go to the hospital later in the day. Upon visiting the hospital I would fake sickness and the doctor would recommend a shot to help. I would have no choice but to receive the shot silently and painfully knowing that I was not sick. The injections were so painful that after a few times I finally gave up on lying and I promised myself that I would never lie again. I embraced the school life from then on. The next time you want to lie and miss school, think of the consequences later in life even if you will not receive shots. Thank you to the doctor because he helped me change my bad habit of faking illnesses to miss school.

CHEAPSKATE ALERT!
ID: 322

I'm a real sucker for discounts and bargains. At a flea market, I was approached by an odd looking man; he told me that he was selling a really cheap laptop. He seemed sincere enough when he told me that he needed the money so he was selling it. This was my first mistake; I did not even ask him where he got the laptop. He asked me to follow him to one of the dark corners of the market, I eagerly followed him. That was my next mistake, for there I saw that there were two other dubious-looking men. I started to back out, but he assured me that I could trust him. Before I could go any further, a friend of mine who also happened to be there stopped me. She asked me why I was following the "creepy looking guy", I told her about the deal I had struck. She explained to me that there were a lot of hawkers who lied to bargain hunters to rob them blind. I was very grateful to my friend for her foresight. I could not imagine what could've happened to me had she not stopped me. Most bargains are not really worth the trouble you go through for them; I learned from this experience that I must evaluate the worth of a certain thing rather than getting blinded by how much of a discount you can get from it.

CHOOSE YOUR BATTLES

ID: 119

My son was four years old. I was in the living room with the other children when I noticed he had been gone for quite some time. I knew he had run upstairs to go to the bathroom so I did not worry much. After about fifteen minutes, I sent one of the other kids up to check on him. They brought down an ink covered little four year old. His sister was grinning from ear to ear so I knew something was up. My little boy looked up and said, "They are my drawers." I was confused and looked to his sister for an explanation. She simply said ," Mom you need to go upstairs." I walked upstairs and looked into his room. Nothing. I looked at the line of children that was following me. My oldest said, "Go look at his dresser. At the time my son shared a dresser with my youngest daughter in another room, so I went to look. There in big bold blue letters was his name, written in marker, across three dresser drawers. I looked at him for an explanation and though he knew he was in trouble all he said was "Look Mom I wrote my name." My anger faded and I remembered an important lesson from my mother to choose your battles with your children. I told him writing his name was good, but why on those drawers? He said it was because those were the drawers his clothes were in. I told him that was a good way to remember but that we did not write on drawers. He was sentenced to attempting to clean his mess which proved futile since he had used a fabric marker, but he has not written on furniture since. So many lessons were learned that afternoon: 1) Do not leave fabric markers within reach, 2) Label drawers with the label maker before your child can, and most importantly 3) Choose your battles wisely and let the punishment fit the crime.

BUYING LOW-PRICED HARDWARE
ID: 498

From a very young age I was fond of changing hardware for my P.C. I was not ok with hardware which grew old to me even after a year. I always wanted to stay updated with the hardware world. But this costs me a lot as the price of hardware isn't cheap. My parents barely provided me with the full cost for my hobby. I had to manage it through different sources. So when my demand got higher than my capacity, I was forced to look into cheaper hardware which was available at my country's illicit market. Many types of updated hardware were sold there for a very reasonable price. Of them, some were also from robbery or theft. One day, I bought the parts of a whole P.C. to assemble a new P.C. as I was getting superb hardware at a very low price. But this P.C. did not last long. Within 3 months I found out about the sever problems and realized that the parts were counterfeit and I had to lose a very handsome amount of money in this deception. From then on, I changed my mind about buying illicit hardware and also put a hold to my excessive mind changing.

SOMETHING SMELLS A LITTLE FISHY...
ID: 57

As a child I would love to go around and play. I would love to play so much that when I needed to go to the bathroom, I would try as hard as I could to hold it in. One day while playing at my house outside, I needed to take a #2,

BUT instead of going inside, I stood in one spot, and flexed my butt muscles as much as I could so that it wouldn't come out. Next thing I know, it starts dripping down my pants... I came inside, and my mom started to yell at me, and so I wasn't allowed to go outside for the rest of the week. Lesson learned: when you need to use the bathroom, smartest choice is to go ahead and use it.

BURN-OUT

ID: 348

I wake up on most days dragging my body off my bed as if the bed were actually resting on my shoulders. Over the past months, absenteeism and punctuality have consistently been my superior's concern about my performance. I've taken enough pain killers to shut down at least one of my kidneys due to recurring tension headaches that none of my doctors could diagnose. All these things led to a burn-out.

I took a few days off so that I could spend time with my family and for myself as well. I tried reflecting on the times that I felt really bad and realized that on days when the headaches were at their worst, I was thinking of one problem after another. I tried to figure out everything, from my family's concerns to the slightest troubles we were having at work. I thought I was Superman. My body thought otherwise. It sent its own stress signals so that I'd ease up. After figuring this out, I stopped. No, I did not let go of my responsibilities. Instead, I began to delegate and train people to step up so that I could just focus on the supervision of more people who were prepared to deal with the small details. I talked to my wife more often so that we could address our concerns together. Only then was I able to breathe again, sleep well again. Problems come and go. But every minute we do not live the way we want, it is a part of our lives we'll never get back.

Mistakes In Life: The Path To Wisdom

BLIND DATE

ID: 2

When I was around 23, I went on my first blind date with someone I had met online. During that whole 2 or 3 months of non-continuous talking he mentioned sharing pictures, but I refused. I thought it would be more fun and exciting to have a good surprise (for both of us). It was a big surprise indeed, but not in a good way. When he walked up to greet me for the first time I froze and felt like my soul just ran the other way screaming for life. The first thought came into my mind was "WOW, Frankenstein does exist!" and I knew I would never forget this first blind date, lol. I decided to be polite and go on the date because I was hoping his personalities would make up for his looks, but nope! I really should have shared pictures and found out more about him before going on that date!!!

LOVE YOUR LIFE

ID: 521

There was a time in my life where I just wanted to end it. A time when I just wanted to jump off a cliff and just disappear. At that time, it was the most responsible thing to do. I thought of escaping from the misery, from the problems, and from the future failures that were ahead of me. I did it once, twice, thrice, it does not freaking work. It's like I have hurt myself for nothing. Then I tried again, it soon resulted as self harm rather than suicide. Then one day I got into a small car accident, I really thought I was going to die, but it's like something had saved me from the wreck. It spared me from any serious injury which was a miracle. Then it hit me, all this time. I've been trying to kill myself because I hate my life. Now I was shaken and awaken to the fact that it's the other way around. I got to reflect and see the beauty instead of the bad. I've got to realize that I was so selfish because I was ending my life and leaving other people to suffer. I realized that in this life there is definitely something that's worth living for, or even just the possibility of something. So, wake up, don't learn this the hard way, help yourself see the beauty of life and start to love your life.

My Lan T. Tran

LOOK BEFORE YOU LEAP

ID: 76

A year ago, I was hired by a multinational call center company. Our batch of newly hired employees was comprised of 10 people and we had undergone process training together. During the training weeks, we do things almost together as a group; the class activities, tests and lunch breaks.

During one of our breaks, my co-worker Jake talked about buying a high-end digital camera with his first pay check, and I said I wanted to buy a laptop. This eventually led to everybody talking about buying something as their reward for getting this job. Suddenly, one of my co-workers, Gina, made a business proposal to us. She stated that she could order the items we wanted from abroad through her aunt who was residing there, with a much cheaper price than our local rate. Everybody was interested in it and asked her for some more details. At first, I shrugged off the idea. However, she had been talking about it for several weeks until she finally had me and Jake convinced. She said that all I needed to do was to make a down payment of $125.00 towards the total price of $375.00 which I thought was a good deal at that time.

To make a long story short, I gave her the money the day I received my first pay check. She assured us that the items would be delivered within a week. A week had passed, then a couple more weeks, then a few months, but we still didn't receive the products. We had done the best that we could to follow up with her, however she had given us almost every alibi she could think of. She even blamed the bad weather as to why they couldn't ship the items and that she couldn't give our money back because her aunt had already purchased the items. Jake had finally decided to notify our HR office of the incident to carry out the necessary actions. Unfortunately, our HR wouldn't intervene with the issue because they said it was a personal concern. Unexpectedly, we heard that she went AWOL. Later, we found out that there were several people who were also victims of her frauds. There were other employees claiming that she borrowed money from them, to which she had not repaid. She is nowhere to be found and our HR department won't even give us her address because it's confidential information.

Mistakes In Life: The Path To Wisdom

Someone once said "trust and you will have true peace", but how can you be at peace if the one you trust is a fraud. What I'm saying is be careful of whom you trust. Some people are only after your money. Some show some good but have a hidden agenda. Now I make sure that I do some checking before I do anything with someone, unless I've known the person all my life. I am skeptical now of things that seem too good to be true. I currently live by the saying "look before you leap".

NEVER COUNT YOUR CHICKENS BEFORE THEY'RE HATCHED

ID: 384

Don't we love it when sometimes it seems as if everything's going our way? With minimal effort, things would just start rolling in our favor as if Lady Luck had suddenly decided to shower us with blessings.

That's exactly how I felt about a year ago when an old associate I worked with on a project called me to ask if I was currently employed. He said a big resort that included a golf course was to be developed near my hometown and they needed an experienced engineer to manage the project. He said he was asked by the general contractor if he knew anyone who was up to the task that was familiar with the area as well. That's when he called me so the three of us could talk. He told me he had a lot of faith in me since I handled his previous contract pretty smoothly for two years before he decided to terminate his services with the company I used to work for. They paid for what I was sure was a very expensive dinner and flattered me all night that I agreed to join the project the next day. That was, of course, after they gave me the figure for my initial salary. I was so blind-sighted by all the sweet talking and flattery that it never occurred to me that when things seem too good to be true, they probably are not. Needless to say, I filed for resignation immediately and went on a break for the next two weeks while they said they'd finalize other details of the project. I tried calling my contact but I never heard from them again.

While I sometimes still feel the need to explain how I came to make this stupid mistake, I never do. The only upside to this story was that during those times, I was still a bachelor at the time which is why there were few bills to pay that could easily be covered by my savings. I found a new job after some time and tried my best to forget about the whole thing. A few months later, I met up with my cousin who was the HR manager for another construction company and my story somehow came up in the conversation. She asked me what the name of the contractor was and laughed after I told her. She said her company worked with that "contractor" a few years earlier. They were blacklisted from most networks after the story spread that they would collect down payments but leave the work behind and often, in very poor condition. She said had I been following the news, I would've heard of the whole thing.

In any big decision, due diligence goes a very long way. Had I put some time into researching the background of those people, I would have saved myself from that mess. Never count your chickens (especially if they're too good to be true) until they're hatched.

WORK VERSUS PERSONAL LIFE TIP #3
ID: 209

Don't work too many hours.

The usual notion in most offices is that the longer the hours you work, the better employee you are. This is totally wrong and I am speaking based on experience.

Back at my first job, I always worked extra hours. Not really because I wanted to impress my boss, but mainly because I wanted ALL TASKS to be completed before I went home. I never even thought about whether the task list I had was really do-able within my 8-hour shift. I just kept on completing all my tasks. A year later, my performance review came and I thought it was unfair because I got some pretty low scores for time management aka finishing tasks on time. I was confused! How the hell did I get a low score like this when I've always met deadlines and I've always completed my task lists. This bothered me for quite some time and so one day, I approached my boss and asked about this item specifically.

Mistakes In Life: The Path To Wisdom

He told me that time management/meeting deadlines is not only about submitting your work on time but more of, managing your time properly and working on the tasks, only within your work hours. Why? Because adhering to your work hours ensures that you are keeping your work-life balance and that you are taking care of yourself to prevent downtime from work. Doing your work within office hours is also a reflection of how you manage time. If you always extend your hours at work, it means there is something wrong: either you are taking too long to complete your work or your task list is really just not do-able in 8 hours. Regardless of the reason, something has to be done to fix it.

Right now, I stay in the office around 10-12 hours, not because of work, but because I take some personal time in between those hours. I proved that keeping my work within just the regular 8 hours has made me less stressed, and more energetic at work. I also found myself no longer complaining about the workload because my working day is always planned out well at least before I get to the office.

WHAT ARE THE FEELINGS OF LONELINESS

ID: 557

I am the youngest of my siblings. I have an elder sister, one year & 9 days older than me. Being the youngest is sometimes good, but sometimes bad too. I was with my family until I finished school and got myself admitted to a college. I remember the time I still lived with my family. Everyone was so careful with me. Can you believe I've never been to the market because of this? Sometimes I was bored too. But after going to college, I realized why we need family. For college I had to leave home. I came to an unknown dazzling city. But I was alone. I felt uneasy to talk to unknown people. So, for the first few months I had no friends, I didn't even know anyone in that town. There was no one to talk to me. Can you imagine any world without friends, without having one? At that time I felt that....& I realized the needs of friends and family. Before that I actually thought I could live all alone.

My Lan T. Tran

Can you imagine how much of a fool I was then? But those few months taught me well about the feelings of loneliness. The best thing I have learned is we need friends, family and a social life to live like a human. And this is why we live in a society, not in forest or cave.

BIG TIME SPENDERS

ID: 232

When I was 16, I got my first car. I was very proud of it and tried to take good care of it (it was actually a piece of junk 1978 Chevy Nova but I treated it as if it were a Rolls Royce). I managed to convince my parents to co-sign me a credit card for "car emergencies". This was a huge mistake. Take note parents: in this day and age, kids have a lot of pressure to be in the nicest of clothes and own all the newest gadgets. I maxed out my credit card within 2 months. While the limit was low because I was 16, it was still very difficult for me to pay off with my part-time job that I only worked 10 hours per week at (for minimum wage, no less). I never did tell my mom that I couldn't handle having a credit card. She noticed that I had a lot of new clothes but I managed to convince herself that it was due to my earnings at my job and that I found really good deals on clothes. The credit card bill came in; I would pay a little bit off and then rack it up again. They kept increasing my limit until I actually had to phone them to get them to stop. I continued on this pattern until the age of 29 when I stopped shopping all together and smartened up. That's 13 years of overspending. Yikes. Knowing what I know now, I would never allow my own kid to get a credit card unless I was certain that they knew how to spend wisely.

Mistakes In Life: The Path To Wisdom

STOP PLEASING PEOPLE – DO WHAT PLEASES YOU!

ID: 420

I have been a doormat to several of my friends since college. No, I am not entirely proud of this description but I just wanted to emphasize being a doormat would not earn the respect of people around me. My friends are so accustomed to the fact that I was their all-around servant. I used to share a house with them and sometimes I would receive text messages from them telling me to collect their laundry, get something for them from across where we live, and so on. Back then I did not mind all of it. But now I must say I have already earned my self-respect and am confident enough to stand up for myself, because I never could remember any single time wherein I was the one who sought favors from them. Maybe except for borrowing their money or some of their clothes, but these were returned as I promised. I was a people-pleaser until I would totally forget about my own needs. I started to realize my dreams and to forget everything in the past. I think it made me more confident in not just taking people's mess and having to solve it for them. Ultimately, I am now at a point of learning where I can say no without ever feeling guilty. I would remind myself, I have my own life and that I am also just as busy as these other people. I am not their pushover friend and servant anymore because I have learned to stand up from all the friendly requests that usually turn into abuse since I never put a stop to them.

SPECULATION IS A GAMBLE

ID: 580

Money makes the world go round, or so it is said. Whatever you want to do must cost you something. It is in this quest that there are numerous times I have put money in baskets in the hope of it doubling or making a profit. When there was an IPO of a company that I believed in, I decided to put up my money in the hope of making money from selling the shares once the share price went up high enough.

Speculation was at its best. I look back and I think I bought the shares because of the hype and I wanted to look all young and independent with knowledge of business. I put up most of my savings for this and as it went, on the opening of the stocks, the share price dropped drastically and 3 years later, it has never gone up to the price at which it was bought.

I learned to do research on more than just what I saw on television as I came to learn the economy's impact on share prices and also speculation is much more of a gamble than actually making a good business decision. I have not recovered that money yet but learned my lesson really hard.

REPORT CARDS
ID: 13

When I was in fifth grade, I was not doing as well as I usually did academically; I had an F in Social Studies when I usually had A's and B's. When the progress report came out, I freaked, and didn't know what I'd do if my mom saw it. I had an idea to put white-out on the grade then write a 90 in its place. When I gave it to my mom, she knew instantly that something wasn't right. I got in BIG trouble at home. It was even worse when I went to school. The teacher did not trust me anymore, and the principal wanted to see my mom. I felt like it was never going to end. Lesson learned: NEVER EVER lie about your education.

THERE ARE TIMES WHEN YOU CANNOT TRUST A DOCTOR
ID: 101

Sometime last year, I had to be on medical leave for around a month because of intolerable colds and cough, and sporadic fever. Around a week of these symptoms, and yet I only self-medicated. On the second week when my health didn't improve, I went to visit a doctor from Healthway

Mistakes In Life: The Path To Wisdom

Clinics in Alabang and was asked to go through several tests, etc. They found out I had acquired asthma somehow, probably due to allergies; whereas the colds was something just viral. Doctor gave me several prescription drugs that I acknowledged. When I was about to leave, the doctor asked if she could take my vital signs, specifically my blood pressure. I didn't think it had anything to do with my cold and cough but then I thought maybe she had a valid reason, especially after seeing the "overweightness" in me. I agreed and she informed me that my BP was actually 140/100 which she said was hypertensive. I was surprised because my BP is usually just 120/90 or 120/80. She said I'm almost hypertensive and asked me if I wanted medication for it. My trusting self said yes, and she gave me two packs of Amlodipine. I asked her how much and she said it is for free because it is a sample, and that I'd just purchase once I consume all 8 tablets.

So I went home, feeling happy that the doctor had a "generous heart." I also thought she was very nice. Around an hour after taking the pills, my head started aching so bad – as if someone was pounding a hammer on my head. I also felt my face become really warm, and I was dizzy. Puzzled and alarmed, I forced myself to read and understand the pamphlet that came with the free pills. Boy was I surprised! Not because it said that one of the effects was severe headache, but because it specifically says that women who are planning to get pregnant SHOULD NOT take the drug! I felt bad and did further research on Google. Yes – the side effect had been mentioned in every article I read. I was so disappointed and terrified that the effects might be extreme on me – I immediately stopped taking the pills.

I asked some good friends and relatives from the medical field and they said it's really nothing to be scared of after taking just one dose of it, but it was a good move to research and stop the pills as the long term effects could really be what is in the medical document.

The story here is not really focused on the drug itself, but on the fact that doctors can commit mistakes too. Ever since this happened, I've always made it a habit to check the informative pamphlet that goes with medicines, or even do research on Google just to give myself assurance that the drug won't affect any other aspect of my health. Other than checking on this medical stuff, I have also always kept myself informed of anything the doctors ask of me to take or do. I always ask why a certain test has to be done, and what the side effects are. Better to be safe than sorry.

LESSON FROM IMPATIENCE MIND
ID: 463

In the premature stage of trading stocks in the capital market, I used to be a very rough trader. I could not loose my temper in trading commodities considering there was a very high magnitude of risk. I was very aggressive in nature even though I was supposed to make every decision from a controlled mind. These problems grounded me with a very high amount of losses in the share market. Not only in the capital market but I also suffered much in my personal life for being this unstable in my mind. I always used to irritate my partners with some of my hasty decision making and changes of mind. I could never be stagnant to a single decision as I always adored changes. But I should've kept it in my mind. People may not love the way I would love to lead my life. When I promised to continue my life with her [my wife], I should have considered her likings as well. If I could have done this, I would have never lost my wife. If I could have learned to have patience, I would have never lost my investments. If I could have controlled myself, I would have never lost myself. So always try to have control over your mind and have patience, because an impatient mind can put your life in the bin.

CHECK ALL OF YOUR THERMOSTATS BEFORE YOU LEAVE FOR VACATION
ID: 285

We woke up a little late for our flight to Mexico. We had already packed but we had to get to the airport. In our haste we didn't check to see if we turned everything off before we left. When we came home two weeks later, our home was very warm. Our hydro bill came a few weeks later and was double what it normally was. Take that extra minute before you leave for vacation to ensure that all of your thermostats are turned down.

BLAME

ID: 42

When I was about 8 or 9 I loved mac and cheese. I still do! But my mom didn't like me having it every day, so I would eat it secretly. One night, she found an unwashed dish filled with leftover cheese, and called my sisters and I down. She asked us who did it, but I was too scared to confess, so I hid behind my older sister. Then after a suspense-filled 5 seconds, my oldest sister took the blame for me, and got in huge trouble. It's no wonder why she sometimes imagines me being murdered... lesson here is confess to your actions!

SAVING THE BEST FOR LAST

ID: 323

Normally I eat half of a foot long turkey sub at work every day. When I buy the sub I ask for some extra banana peppers 'cause I LOVE LOVE LOVE them. I would eat the first half of the sub with 30% of those extra peppers leaving 70% for the next day, thinking I was saving the best for last. So on Monday this week, I ate the first half. The second half, that I left in the common fridge at work, had a ton of those peppers that I was looking forward to eating on Tuesday. Tuesday's lunch came along and I went to the fridge and the second half of my sub was no where to be seen. I searched all over and it was nowhere to be found. I was not happy. Someone either threw it away or ate it. I learned my lesson, always eat the good stuff first 'cause anything can happen the next minute/day, especially when you share a fridge with other people. Kind of like when someone says, "life is short, eat dessert first."

My Lan T. Tran

BE CAREFUL ABOUT JOKES ON AGE
ID: 121

My husband is twenty years older than me, and so jokes about old age and immaturity always come into play when we are teasing each other. Whenever he forgets something, I always tell him that he either has a "memory gap," or "signs of old age," or "Alzheimer's symptoms." In the same light, he also teases me about being "immature," "childish," or "retarded" whenever I do something wrong. There was never an instance that we felt bad about these jokes.

One night while cleaning the house, we both stumbled upon an unopened DVD case of the movie, "The Notebook." My husband isn't a fan of love stories, nor dramas, so I was really puzzled that he was insistent on watching this. I can't write about the whole story, but in case you want to know more, check this out > http://en.wikipedia.org/wiki/The_Notebook_(film).

Anyway, we both cried while watching the movie. We were silent a few minutes after the movie ended, and then proceeded to the usual midnight snack and started living our normal "funny" lives.

Two nights ago, almost a month after we watched the movie, my husband had vodka night with my cousin. He was drunk after just over two hours of drinking. He was way too far from his normal self – noisy, annoying, laugh-tripping. I didn't want him to wake the rest of the household up... so, I insisted we just go to bed. (It was 3 AM after all!) As I was just about to doze off, my husband started crying. He told me: "Dear, if one day I wake up not knowing who you are, please promise me that you'd still take care of me, and be patient with me. But if things go worse than memory problems, or if I can't contain myself, or if I can't even control my own poop, please think about just letting off my life. I don't want you to suffer any hardships taking care of me." He was crying the whole time he was saying this, and I was overwhelmed with emotion. I felt guilty while thinking about the times I teased him about "Alzheimer's." I cried with him through the night. I said sorry for being insensitive about his age, and for throwing jokes about old age. I said I was sorry if he felt that I couldn't take care of him. We fell asleep crying.

Mistakes In Life: The Path To Wisdom

Surprisingly, this small incident changed the way I look at life, especially the upcoming years with my husband. I realized I love him even more now, and that I should be more sensitive of his feelings. And even if he is my husband, I'd say that the usual adage still holds – respect the elderly.

SHARP TONGUE, HARSH WORDS

ID: 500

I have a tendency to speak quite frankly and harshly towards my friends. It's not that I am mean or anything, it's just the way I talk with people I'm used to. I think I might have gotten this harshness from my father. I don't swear as much as him but still, I speak very bluntly. There was one day, honestly I was just kidding around with my friend. My friends should know how I am, they even told me once "I bet if I didn't know you, I'd be crying by now." It was a joke but still mixed with some truth. Well, I was teasing my friend but I guess it reached the point where she did cry. It honestly took me by surprise. First of all, she was my friend. Secondly, she cried because of me. I had too much pride back then, so I never said I was sorry because I wasn't. It was not intentional, and I was a bit annoyed as well. I don't really know what she was thinking. I didn't know if there was some deeper reason but I just let it pass with time like I always did. Sometimes I am unaware of the way people can receive my words. Just because it means something innocent and friendly to me, it doesn't mean it will be accepted in the same way by another. So I tried to moderate my words a bit by thinking before I speak. Yes, I don't speak that harshly anymore but I can't change myself completely. This sharp tongue of mine is something I have used for years now. Right now, I'm just trying to carefully choose the people I wield this weapon on.

My Lan T. Tran

HATE FOR MATHEMATICS

ID: 58

When I was in grade 7, I hated mathematics so much that I wouldn't do assignments given by the teacher. Because I knew the teacher would walk around the class checking if assignments had been done, I would sneak out of class and hide in the bathroom. I did this several times until the teacher noticed my absence record and asked the rest of the pupils if I was in school. The students were ordered to come and get me from the toilet and contrary to what I expected, the teacher asked me what my problem was and I explained to him that I hated mathematics and that I was always afraid I'd be punished for not doing the assignments. The teacher was understanding and promised to give me more attention on the subject. He also promised that I would end up liking the subject like the rest of the students. I started doing better and asking questions on things that I didn't understand. I learned that nothing is difficult as long us one has a positive attitude. The teacher helped me change my attitude and I became the best student in mathematics for the rest of my years in school.

NO RUSH

ID: 351

One of my good friends decided that they wanted to set me up with one of their friends a few years ago. I was pretty happy being single and enjoying my life the way it was but I figured what the heck, how bad can it be? I talked with Dave on the phone a few times, and he seemed nice enough, so I went to hang out with a couple of his friends and him. That evening went alright, nothing too weird, just a group of friends laughing and having a good time. Since that night wasn't so bad, when Dave asked me to come over and watch a movie with him I went. Nothing bad happened when I went, but I started to get really weird vibes from him. He lived at home with his mom, even though he had a really good job and his own car. And when I met her she seemed really excited to meet me. We watched a movie on two different nights before stuff really got weird. He started talking about how happy he was with me being his girlfriend, and how his mom was really excited and had even offered to let me move in with them.

I was completely freaked out. It had only been like four or five "dates" where we hung out and watched movies. I think we had only kissed once or twice. I was definitely not his girlfriend in my mind, and was not ready for that with anyone, much less someone who wanted me to move in with his mom! I had to let Dave know that this was not the place I was in with my life, but that we were better off as friends. I learned a valuable lesson from that experience. I learned to pay attention to others reactions to me a little closer, and I learned that if it isn't broken, don't fix it! I was happy being single, and I didn't need to rush a relationship at that time.

BE SENSITIVE TO YOUR EMPLOYEES – PART 2

ID: 145

Employee #2 – my team member.

I work as a Helpdesk Manager. My team offers technical assistance to customers who purchased our software. As you may know, this type of work requires a high level of technical skill, compliance to tight deadlines, and not to mention, a focused and consistent work ethic.

My team is great. I hire people in an unconventional manner though – I don't hire the highly technical people, I don't hire experts, I don't hire geniuses... I hire people-oriented applicants, who are eventually given the title: Application Engineer. Weird huh? The strategy has worked really well though – I have happy customers, who always provide feedback around how my team cannot only solve problems, but are able to establish relationships and trust with them.

The strongest member of my team in terms of connecting to customers is this employee #2 I am talking about today. Whenever he is on the phone with a customer, he often goes beyond his target talk time, because the customer loves talking to him. When in team gatherings, he is the one who breaks the ice, making everyone laugh. He is very good at teasing our gay team member (who does not really mind – he actually likes being made fun of). He leads events planning and get-togethers. He is our "Ace Ventura."

Two months ago, we noticed a 180 degree change. Employee #2's presence was almost never felt in the office – he was either absent, or present but disengaged. I tried to talk stuff out during our weekly one-on-one's but he kept on saying he was okay and was just busy. "Being busy" did not reflect in his statistics though. He rarely picked up on tickets, he didn't answer his phone, he literally was not working.

I was so stupid – I should have just taken some time to look on Facebook. His fiancée just called their engagement off! Worst of all– on Facebook! I guess I couldn't perfectly describe how he was feeling about this, and how he was taking this. But I can imagine that if I felt devastated by it… what about him? They had been together for seven years, and now this?

I called him to my office the day after. I told him upfront that I needed to know why he has been acting this way, and from there, he just burst into tears! I was speechless. He started to tell me stuff – how this affected his work, and how being in the office helped him cope. I was torn in between keeping him in his normal schedule, or putting him to the graveyard shift. The rest of the team was getting annoyed with his work attitude, but I couldn't tell them about his personal problem. I then just put him on the graveyard shift, where he had to work either alone, or with just one person (who was also aloof to him). I let this go on for about a month, but I didn't see an improvement.

Last week, I had to call him to my office again. He literally begged me to put him back to his usual shift. I told him to justify, and he said he really needed to be with a team because he felt alone. He found the team to be the second most important support system he had, next to his family and that by simply being with us, he felt relief and assurance that he would be able to move on soon. A lot of talk went on and I realized, just like that of Employee #1 (the driver) — that I had been insensitive to others' feelings.

While my job required me to stick to policies and processes, I should have, in this instance, applied the "humane" aspect in my decision-making. I should have thought about what I could have done to help him cope, instead of forcing him to do what I thought was best for him. While he would have gone through the misery, he would have done so in an easier manner had I helped him and had I asked the team to support him as well.

Mistakes In Life: The Path To Wisdom

I hope I am not too late. I decided to put him back onto the regular day shift schedule where he could interact with the team, but at the same time I asked him to compromise to put his work ethic back and to try to be as open as possible as to how we can help him further.

He starts his day shift tomorrow, and I really hope it's going to be the start of his better days.

DON'T WASTE YOUR TIME

ID: 523

All of us know "Time and Tides wait for none". But actually only a few use their time properly. Most of us waste time or don't care about time. When I was much younger, I was lazy & ruthless. I didn't do anything timely. I was always late for everything and this didn't bother me. I never did my homework or study at the due times. All day I was just making leisure time. As a result, my grades were always lower than most of the other students in my class. I also failed to get admitted to any better college. One day my Dad talked to me about my situation and soon he realizes my problem. That day he talked to me for a long time and taught me about the importance of time maintaining in life. He taught me that you could never succeed in life unless you go with the time. And that conversation really influenced me. Though I was admitted to an average college, now I am a student of one of the famous engineering institution of my country. I have reached here only by working hard and time maintaining, although I am not extra ordinarily bright.

ALWAYS KNOW WHERE THE ROUTE IS

ID: 78

Years back, I moved to a new city because of a job opportunity. Since I was not yet familiar with the exact route to my office, I rode a cab to get to work on time. Because I only had 20 minutes before work started, I told the driver that I was in a hurry and told him the exact name of the company and the exact address. The cab driver then nodded to me and drove on. Usually, it would only take 15-20 minutes travel from my place to work if I rode a taxi cab. About 30 minutes later, I was still in the cab and wondering why the buildings were not quite familiar. Somewhat annoyed and nervous because I was already late and didn't know where I was at, I asked the taxi driver why it was taking so long to get to my work place.

He then finally admitted that he was also new to the place and that there were just a few times that he had gotten lost. He tried to ask me if I knew where the route was to my office but unfortunately I was not of any help either because I didn't even know where the hell we were at that moment.

Later, we ended up stopping and asking passersby for the right way. In the end, I was one hour late for work and already exhausted for the day.

I learned a very significant lesson from that day; to make sure that I know the exact, shortest or safest route to where I am going. So guys, please remember the buildings, landmarks or street signs you are passing by. If it's your first time going to the place, ask directions from someone who has been there or better yet bring a map.

THREE'S A CROWD

ID: 374

I cheated on my relationship once. It started the way most of these things happen — friendly conversations, casual meet-ups, and other similar seemingly innocent schemes. The first lie we often tell ourselves is that it's nothing serious. That it's all a harmless game, a gauge of how "marketable" we still are despite the few pounds we've gained. A few encounters later and we found ourselves deeper and deeper into the situation.

My case was a little more complicated since I had a kid with my first girlfriend. I often told the girl I cheated with that I was only trying to protect the child that's why I kept my relationship with his mother. She believed the lie each time. I lived the lie for two years. By that time, my

Mistakes In Life: The Path To Wisdom

conscience bothered me so much that I eventually told her that we shouldn't see each other anymore. For weeks she begged me to take her back until it suddenly stopped. Just when I thought everything was over, my girlfriend called me one day to ask me how long I've been broken up with the other girl. I was stunned. I couldn't give her a straight answer and I apologized incessantly like my life depended on it. For days she wouldn't even answer my calls and on those few times she did, she'd make it obvious how cold she felt towards me. I courted her for months until she finally gave in and agreed to put everything in the past. Despite this, I knew that our relationship would be marred for life.

There is no hidden message in my story. The lesson is quite obvious, "never betray someone's trust". It's a very practical advice. The temptations, they will always be there. What's important is to remember that while some things may be fixed, there are some others that, when taken for granted, can never be taken back.

COUNT THE CHANGE BEFORE LEAVING

ID: 197

I was shopping for grocery items once at a very busy time of the day and needed to line up in a long queue. My shopping cart was nearly half full of grocery items to last me two weeks. The cashier lady was obviously so busy too that she barely looked at the people around her or to the customer she was serving. She only did this when it was time to take the payment. She seemed very efficient in handling the punching and the cash register. She could quickly finish a whole cart full of items, could easily process the payment and give the change back seamlessly. I was paying cash that time and was confident enough that I had made the transaction without a hitch. However, when I was about to give a tip to the store guy who helped carry my items to the car, I wondered why I was short of cash.

I counted the coins and found out that I was shortchanged. Because of this, I needed to go back to the cashier again, disturbing the long line of people, and asked for the correct change.

My Lan T. Tran

It is really true that "you need to count your change before leaving."

WHY SHOULD WE NEED TO OBEY OUR PARENTS

ID: 558

Parents have given birth to us and give us a chance to see the beautiful earth. They took care of us when we were young and weak. We also learned the world from them. They are the guide of our young age and the last hope for us.

I was raised with a lot of love; my life was easy to me as my parents helped me with everything. Although my parents loved me so much, I didn't obey them when I was younger. I chose a different path than the path they asked me to go. It was like if they said go left, I went every way except left.

By doing this type of stuff I was lost in my life. I had bad company and habits, which was ruining my future. But my parents didn't give up on me. They tried their best to bring me back to a normal life. With their help, at last I figured out my life. And I also figured out that our parents only want our own success for us. So now I obey them and try to do what they want me to do.

WATER IS GOOD FOR THE BODY BUT...

ID: 234

... take it conscientiously especially when traveling.

I think I am addicted to water now. I have made it a point to drink at least eight glasses of water at work, plus another 4-8 at home, depending on whether it is a weekday or a weekend. I found it to be good for my health.

Mistakes In Life: The Path To Wisdom

I've lost some weight because of water therapy, and I no longer feel dehydrated when under the sun.

This practice of drinking water has always served me well, until, one time, when I had to take the bus going to my hometown, instead of driving. I didn't even realize that it was a 6-hour trip and so I just went on my usual "hobby" of drinking water. Around three hours after I boarded the bus, I felt the need to pee and this felt like it was one of those I-can-not-hold-this-anymore times. I really had to go! There were, however, no bus stops nor toilets in sight so I tried to control it until it got to the point where I was almost shivering and perspiring at the same time because of the pain I was feeling. I don't know how long this took, but, luckily (just for me), the bus had a flat tire. Oh glorious! We had to stop by a gasoline station, and I literally just scrambled out the door and ran towards the first toilet-looking area I could see. That was like one of the best moments of my life. Lol.

I don't remember what happened after that, like, if people actually noticed me… but one thing got to me: just because something is good....doesn't mean you have to do it all the time.

DON'T BE A FOOL

ID: 422

When I was in high school, I really made a fool of myself a lot and made fun of other people, especially with my classmates. There was a time when I threw chewing gum in my classmate's hair. She really cried and told our teacher what happened. I was suspended for a week because of this. On the other hand, I was a bit happy because I had lots of time to stroll around. However, things didn't happen the way I wanted, my parents grounded me to my room. I was so sad and very lonely for about a week because I had no one to talk to. I realized that it is really hard to be alone, and doing some foolishness will just lead you to an unhappy life. So friends, it is really important to do the right and good things to other people.

My Lan T. Tran

THINK TWICE

ID: 582

Life is full of ups and downs and till now I have passed very hard situations like any other person and also the good life paths. When I was a second year college student, my courage of studying for a long time was very high. When the mid exam was approaching, all students (including me) were studying very hard to score better results. The mid exam schedule was outlined on board. I was so tense that I didn't see the schedule. Nevertheless, my friends told me the sequence of courses that we would take. According to the schedule, we took exams for most of the courses. At that time I was living outside the university so that after each exam, I directly went home. The tragic started at this time; The exam time of the final course was rescheduled from 9 PM to 8 AM. I didn't hear that but my friends repeatedly called me but I didn't want to waste my time and didn't answer the phone rather continue reading the course without going to the library. On the next day, I went to the exam hall based on the old schedule. When I went into the room no one was there. I asked myself, 'Where are they?' A mix of ideas was flowing into my mind... and I called one of my friends, "Hi Mat, what is the matter with the students... nobody is here... why didn't you come... did the schedule time change?" He shouted, "I tried to get you on the phone but you didn't answer...the exam was in the morning..." I threw the phone and cried...

On the next day, I told to my Survey teacher that I missed the exam. He was a nice person and politely said "you will take the exam soon but bear in mind that in exam days, don't be careless and not only stick to studying... you have to get the latest information..." Since then during the exam days, I have been up to date with new information.

LIFE IS CHANCES

ID: 17

When I was about 18 to 21 years old, I made many mistakes in school. I used to hate the teachers, students and everyone around me. I used them as an excuse to hate school and to not study, thinking it was a waste of time and no good could come from it. Forcing myself to believe I was living a life I didn't choose, I didn't see why I should care about it. Forgetting that this life is the only one I have and that every step or mistake I make will affect my future! So I kept fooling around and got in all kinds of trouble in school instead of studying and getting good grades to be able to travel and change the life I had... So now I realize not only did I waste the chance to become better but I was also 3 years behind the other students in the class. Realizing that I am older than all of them makes me sad.

But now I realize that success won't come without troubles. As hard as your life is, you can't keep complaining about how life is treating you, you should find your path without crying for help, because no one will help you if you can't help yourself. I could have made my life better by thinking positive, instead of making myself the victim of everything.

I learned that life gives many chances. You just have to learn how to take them. Don't expect any change to come if you won't work for it.

CHANGE COMES FROM WITHIN
ID: 102

My workmate came to work crying one day, rumbling about how her boyfriend was treating her like a rag. She said that he always promised her not to have any connection with any girl again but she always caught him smooching with someone else. The previous night in a bar with her friends, they saw him with someone else again. My friend said that she didn't bother to confront her boyfriend anymore and what she did was picked up a guy, got drunk and enjoyed herself. I was about to reprimand her that what she did was not appropriate and she wouldn't be respected as a proper woman and that it was about time to let go of him because he will only ruin her future. But this time, I didn't dare to say anything. I just listened to her, though I have listened to this similar story for the past months. My friend had caught her boyfriend being disloyal several times already but whenever he would come to her and beg for her forgiveness, she would just easily accept him again. Then, she would know of his wrongdoings, dump him and take him back again. It's the same cycle of events every time. My friend won't listen to any sound advice from anyone. She would pretend to for several days, however she would shrug off the idea as soon as her boyfriend made peace with her. That's not even the worst part of their relationship. He always asked for money from her and sometimes would beat her if she couldn't give him any. He has also been rumored to use drugs. And I think the fault here is on my friend. She may not control her boyfriend but she can control her own life. She can break up with him and start a new life. She can even find another boyfriend anytime, one that deserves her love and care. However, no matter how we advise her, she just seems to let it in one ear and out the other.

I realized that you really cannot demand another person to change. I learned that change really comes from within. If someone wants to change for the better, the decision should truly come from them for it to be real. No matter how much I advise my friend to start a new life without her boyfriend, if she hasn't made up her mind about it, my concern for her is still no use.

LESSON FROM OVER OPTIMISM

ID: 466

Optimism is considered a virtue for a man because it drives us to try things we'd never think we'd accomplish. It will make your mind desperate to run for a goal until you accomplish it. But over optimism can lead you to trouble. I was overly optimistic a few years back. I used to be excessively possessive about achieving everything in my life. Let me give an example about my academic life. I was supposed to be the sole student of my class who came from an English version of education in my university. I looked down on everyone, thinking that I was far more advanced than other students because I was from a superior class and background. I used to study very little and passed my time on other things rather than studying. But at the end of the year, I was very angered to have found out that my grade was below the average for the class. I could not justify the reason because I thought I performed well in the exam hall. Gradually I began to understand there were far better students in the class who didn't show

Mistakes In Life: The Path To Wisdom

their strengths. I kept cursing my luck and my over optimistic mentality that led me toward that grading.

So never degrade anyone as your competitors can turn out to be much more functioning and valuable.

DON'T LOAN YOUR 16-YEAR-OLD THE CAR

ID: 293

When I was 16 I was like most other teenagers: obsessed with what other people thought of me. When I first got my driver's license I was the first of my friends to do so and this gave me quite a bit of power. Of course, I wanted to show off in the car all the time – blasting the music, speeding and taking corners too quickly. I learned my lesson one day when I had a girlfriend in the car and we started singing at the top of our lungs to a Beatles song. I wasn't paying attention and all of a sudden – SMASH! I hit the person in front of me – HARD. My friend damaged her knees on the dashboard, I suffered from whiplash and the worst part – the person in front of me was a snobby high school girl's father. So embarrassing. Anyway, my mother's car was written off and 15 years later (15 accident-free years, I might add), my mother still hesitates when I need to borrow her car. If you trust your teenager enough to drive your car that is great, but make sure you set boundaries (such as no friends in the car, no blaring music, etc.)! Some are not as lucky as I was to have escaped alive.

CHEATING

ID: 44

I helped a guy I liked for two years on a test once. I was finished with the test, but he wanted the bonus so he asked me what inch was in Spanish. I tried to show him my binder without looking suspicious but apparently it was so obvious that my teacher yelled at us right away. She lectured the two of us in front of the whole class. It was so humiliating. Since we never did anything wrong in her class before, she let us off the hook but I never cheated for him or any other guy ever again.

MY PHONE'S BATTERY DIED

ID: 324

After a couple of years, I was excited to take a vacation to my hometown and planned to wake up very early to be on the first bus. Everything was packed and ready the day before. However, on the day of the travel, I was disappointed to have known that the first bus had left early and that I had to wait another hour for the next one. But then my hubby who accompanied me to the bus station needed to leave for work and advised me to just call him if I was already on the bus. The bus finally arrived after an hour and when I was about to call my hubby, the phone died. I tried turning the phone on but the battery went off even if I just tried texting. It was a very long ride for both me and my hubby because he was extremely concerned as to why I had not contacted him nor could I be contacted.

After that, I always check my phone for the battery and always fully charge it whenever I plan to go out or away from home.

WALLS HAVE EARS

ID: 122

I have proven it. Walls do have ears. My roommate and I were talking once about how the other tenant across our room is very aloof from the others. She doesn't talk to anyone in our boarding house. We tried to smile at her in the living room and had asked her to join us during our free time however she always ignored us. We talked about how we know so little about her. My friend blurted out that she may be a member of a cult of some sort or a witch perhaps. We both had fun speculating bad things

Mistakes In Life: The Path To Wisdom

about her but managed to keep our voice low to make sure she couldn't hear us.

The next day, while on my way to the kitchen, I came across her. She looked at me directly, approached me and self-assuredly said that she was definitely not a witch or a wicked goblin but just an ordinary girl who has 3 jobs and works 15 straight hours a day with inadequate time for rest. She said that as much as she wanted to join us, she couldn't because she needed all the free time to get herself some sleep. She said that she needed to work hard to send some money for her sick mother because they don't have any other family to help but just the two of them. That she is not fortunate enough to be blessed with a good life like the ones we have. I was teary-eyed after I heard her story and I apologized deeply to her. After that conversation, my friend and I befriended her. If we have a chance, we let her join us while we take our meal. We also give some extra things to her once in a while, groceries, and extra clothes. She's part of our group now and she is the coolest and jolliest person we have ever known in the boarding house.

I also make sure not to judge the person based on my initial perception and not to bad mouth about anyone I haven't gotten the chance to really know.

A BEACON LEADING THE WAY FOR THE RIGHT PATH

ID: 502

This must be the greatest mistake I've ever made, ruining my life and my daughter's future. Due to the annulment I had, I was entirely lost. I was petulant and most of all I was becoming meaner to my daughter. I always hit her even though she had done nothing wrong. My life was completely miserable at that time, so I decided to stay away from my hometown. I transferred to the metropolitan city, leaving my little girl to my parents.

I was able to find a job in the city; however, my salary was not enough to support my daughter, I couldn't even go home any time I wanted because I couldn't afford the expenses. As a result I only went home during special occasions. I never expected that by doing that, my daughter would begin to hate me. The only thing that I noticed is that she never talked to me every time I was home.

Years passed by, my daughter became the lady I expected. But when I went home I was shocked when my mother told me that she turned out to be bisexual. I was shocked and furious, again; I could not accept it. However, my mother told me that was the result of leaving her. If only I was there to guide her then she would never be like that.

I confronted my daughter, but she was very mad at me, she poured out all of her pent up feelings ever since the separation happened and blamed me for that. I was not able to utter even a single word because what she was saying was all true; and worse of all I could never take away the hatred inside her heart. She was also like me to some degree, it was just like history repeating itself; I hated my father now my daughter hated me.

When I went back to the city my heart was so heavy, I couldn't keep myself from crying, and wished if only I could turn back time I would repair all of the mistakes I had done in my life just to save my daughter's future. She was rebellious, dropped out of school, and in short she's ruining her life just to make me realize I made a mistake by leaving her and getting married again.

Now, I'm back in my hometown and trying to win back my daughter's affection. Somehow I know deep within her, a child is still longing for her mother. I am wishing and praying that one of these days our life will be back to normal.

Lesson: As mothers we should never leave our children no matter how difficult our journey will be. We are the light to their path and therefore must be their beacon leading them to the right direction.

Mistakes In Life: The Path To Wisdom

FRAUD

ID: 59

A couple years ago, I worked for a milling company and I had the opportunity to know and interact with several clients. I could tell which customers were good to deal with and those that were bad payers. When I changed my job and moved to another company, one of the clients I knew in the earlier job approached my new employer in order to buy goods from them on a credit account. I was quick to put in a good word for the client because I knew the client was a good payer. A credit account was opened for the client and they started purchasing goods on credit. When the invoices were overdue for payment, I called the client to collect the payment. The client said that they had no account with our company and at no time had they purchased goods from us. I learned that the supposed client was an imposter and had faked the documents for the client I knew. It was at that point we figured out that our company had been conned. Because of this, I lost my well paying job. I learned that there are imposters that can fake anything to get what they want. My advice is that you go the extra mile to verify if you are dealing with the real person or an imposter.

THE ONE THAT GOT AWAY 2

ID: 354

I was browsing through the website and found a post that had the title The One That Got Away and I thought, don't we all have a similar story?

She was my first girlfriend. We didn't even like each other at first. I thought she was boring. She thought I was a snob. I met her through her older sister who I was actually crushing on. We were sort of friends so right before she graduated from high school (yes, we were that young) she said maybe I could look after her sister. The rest was history.

From not liking each other, we ended up texting for hours or until we both ran out of phone credits. During classes we wrote silly love letters, made the craziest promises. We thought we could actually conquer the world together like they did in the movies, only to find out that poor plots lead to unhappy endings. We broke up, went our separate ways. I left for college, she migrated with her family. We dated different people and shared some stories about each. We tried communicating with each other online to the point that I'd stay up late when she was just waking up on another side of the globe. The feelings were still there, we both knew it. The only thing that kept us from each other was the distance between us — thousands of miles of land and sea. Slowly, we gave up on the correspondence, leaving only a short friendly message every once in a while. She got married, I had a kid. We tried sounding casual the few times we chatted online but we never really talked about it. Then the casual conversations stopped altogether.

My regret is not that I didn't try to make a thousand-mile relationship work. Other factors would have weighed in that could have altered the ending to such an attempt. What I regret the most is the fact that I was not honest with her or with myself. How many great loves are there in a lifetime that when one comes, we let the chance to admit it slip away? I should've told her. We may not have ended together but at least, I would've gotten the closure I needed. Now, I only wish her happiness.

DON'T BELIEVE EVERYTHING YOU SEE ON TV

ID: 160

There was an advertisement on the radio and on TV years ago about a facial cream that dramatically eliminates wrinkles and provides clearer and smoother skin. I was enticed by the commercial seen on the TV because of their featured living testimony of the people who were using the cream. They showed photos of themselves illustrating how they looked before and after they used the product. After a week of seeing the ad, I finally decided to try it. I thought it would be good to have much smoother and fairer skin. Unfortunately, after using it a couple of days, I felt that my skin peeled off severely and that I looked like I had the worst sun burn on the face. My face looked very reddish and patchy.

Mistakes In Life: The Path To Wisdom

It was not a pleasant experience at all. The cream made my skin look terrible rather than make it better. After that, I never tried any new cosmetics only heard or seen from the ads. I make sure it really works, has been already tested and used by a friend or a person I know.

DON'T JUDGE A PERSON

ID: 530

I had a classmate in college who was very intelligent and a little bit boastful and arrogant. Everyone in our class hated him. But the time came that he talked to us, went out with us, hung out with us. I thought that he was not who we thought he was; maybe we were just being judgmental and jealous. Then when we graduated, he was the one who helped and encouraged us to find work. I felt ashamed of myself because the person whom I hated the most is the one who helped me. That's it; we should not judge a person.

IS THIS SALT IN MY COFFEE?

ID: 80

I have a set of container bottles with different colored caps for variety of spices and seasonings at home. I put them all in a single kitchen cabinet. One time, still sleepy from a very early morning call, I decided to make myself a cup of coffee to perk up the day. Warm from the coffee maker, I poured some liquid in my glass. Then, with my half-eyes closed, I reached for a bottle with what looked like white sugar in it. I put a considerable amount of the powder in my glass, stirred the coffee and straightly made a big gulped of it. I'm sure you can imagine what my face looked like when I realized I had put refined salt in my coffee. After that, I learned to label each of the bottles corresponding to what's inside them. And I never made the same mistake again.

My Lan T. Tran

GAME ZOMBIE

ID: 388

For a time, I became so hooked on the popular pc game Plants Vs. Zombies. So much so that it consumed all of my free time, I played it even during my office hours. I wasn't getting enough sleep from playing it until the wee hours of the night, sometimes stumbling into bed past 6 a.m.

This situation became a daily routine that it began to affect other aspects of my life. I frequently came to work late and sometimes called in sick because I was too sleepy to go to work. My relationships suffered too. I lied to my friends about not being able to join them in our weekly night out because I only wanted to play the game. My boss complained about the quality of my work output and sometimes I couldn't even meet the deadlines he set.

Finally, my friends decided to hold an intervention session for me. They enumerated what things I missed by playing a computer game instead of being with them. They also asked me if the game was worth the things I was sacrificing in real life. I was shocked. I couldn't believe that a simple game had caused this much damage to my social life. Sometimes I get so engrossed over a particular thing, in this case a game, that it made me overlook the more important and real things in my life.

For sure there are those of you who like playing computer and internet-based games. You may not realize it, but these games can take up most of your time. That time should be spent more profitably and in the company of others.

A LESSON ON OVER-SERVING

ID: 199

A few weeks ago I had friends over to watch a movie. We drank cocktails and ate some home-cooked food. I thought everyone was okay to drive home but didn't consider that the drinking-driving laws here only allow for a .05 blood alcohol level. One of my girlfriends went through a road block and blew over the limit. She had her vehicle impounded, got arrested and lost her driver's license for 3 months. Next time, I will make sure that everyone is safe to drive before leaving my house because not only is this an expensive lesson for her, but I could be found liable under Canadian law since I was the host! It's not worth the risk!

When you have friends over for a few drinks, PLEASE make sure they get home safe. They could lose more than just their license.

DON'T THINK ABOUT ONLY YOU, THINK ABOUT THE WORLD TOO

ID: 560

I was selfish, arrogant and reckless. I cared about no one except me. I had a belief that you are on your own. But that was not correct. Because if that were true, then why do we live with family, why do we live in a society, why do we work in groups, why do we have friends? If everyone is on his own, then no society or family or anything would form. If our mothers thought that, they wouldn't give birth or raise us. Our fathers would not take care of us. Even the scientists would not allow us to use their inventions and the great people like Jesus, Mohammad, Moses or Nelson Mandela would not suffer to show mankind their way and rights. When I realized that, I took a vow; I must try my best to do something for my country and the world. Although I know I cannot do such a great thing, I will try my best.

LOVING TOO MUCH

ID: 239

My husband and I love animals very much. We thought we would be okay living in a condo that only allowed one cat even though we had two. The state by-laws said that we would get fined if we violated any of the laws, of which a limit to animal ownership was one. We couldn't resist. Two cats simply weren't enough. We bought a third. This would have been okay if the new boy looked even remotely like the other two (if he did, people would see him in the window and just assume it was the same cat).

The problem with this theory is that we have nosy neighbors and our living room has a giant window that faces the courtyard. In the courtyard is a tree that houses many birds. So of course our cats spend all day on the windowsill watching the birds, assuming that they will be able to permeate through glass and eat one someday. One of the other neighbors spotted two cats in the window (just two – phew) and we were busted. We were slapped with a hefty fine, told to get rid of a cat (which is absolutely out of the question) and now we have our condo listed for sale. On the bright side, we get to move into a house with a yard.

So the moral of the story is: if you love animals as much as my husband and I do, don't kid yourselves that you will be able to stop at just one. Also, don't assume that your neighbors will turn a blind eye! Save yourself the hassle and move into a house.

LOVE OF PARENTS

ID: 429

I cut classes most of the time. My parents didn't know about this because they were always busy. They thought that I was a good and very diligent student. When the report cards were released, my parents were so shocked and angry because of my failing grades. They blamed themselves for what had happened to me. I was so guilty because they didn't even try to scold me, instead they just let me realized how much they cared for me and for my future. I was really touched by the love that my parents showed me. I realized that they do care and what they're doing is for my future. For you to give back their love, you must do your best to make them happy.

Mistakes In Life: The Path To Wisdom

DISASTER PARTY

ID: 583

As years have gone by I have made many friends and at some point I thought it would be nice if I could put all my friends under one roof. I invited friends from high school and also those I had grown up with in neighborhood. My parents were excited about the party but as usual there were house rules I had to adhere to so as to make my party what I had envisioned.

The day arrived and my birthday party was to be that which would be spoken about for the next few years. I rode with the fact that I was popular in each circle and I was sure of my friends in different circles liking each other. The day went as planned, most of my friends did come and I had games lined up with a hope of mingling people. It is here that the disaster happened, there were those who thought the games I had lined up were boring and the music selection was bad, the food would have done better with more variety and so on.

The envisioned party of all my friends liking each other ended up more of a disaster party. Most of my friends hated the crowd I had invited. Looking back I realize that it goes beyond just bringing people together. It is about getting people with the same interests in the same room and ensuring that their interests are catered for.

BLIND DATE #2

ID: 19

Some time has passed since my first blind date (ID # 2). One day I announced to my friends that work has slowed down and that I wanted to go on dates again. One friend quickly contacted me, saying she found someone awesome for me and would introduce us when we go out clubbing. I said "sure" and got really excited, thinking this one must be a good one because a friend was hooking me up this time. I got to the club and I can still remember vividly when I first looked at him. I immediately looked back at my friend with a smile, the kind of smile that comes with a thought "I'M SOOO GONNA KILL YOU FOR THIS." I swear I have never had such a desire to strangle someone as bad as that night, lol. The date looked like the brother of the Frankenstein I went on a blind date with some time back. I spent an entire night trying to remember what horrible thing I ever did to my friend to have such a terrible hook up like this. But then I remembered how that particular friend of mine would date just about anybody and that I had been so busy working that I hadn't seen her in forever. So neither one of us remembered exactly enough about each other to know what we preferred in dates. Lesson learned: Keep in touch with friends, be mindful of the friend who is playing the match maker, and find out more about the date before going on the date.

GREEN IS HOT

ID: 103

When I was in college I visited a friend in New Mexico. I had never been more than a few states from my home so a trip to New Mexico was like visiting another world. I was lucky enough to stay on an Indian reservation with some of the nicest people I have ever met. I got the opportunity to sit in on classes with some of the most beautiful children I have ever seen because the friend I was visiting was a teacher. As amazed as I was at all the youngsters, they were equally amazed with me as I was one of a very few white people they had ever seen. New Mexico was truly amazing in sight, but I also greatly enjoyed the food. I am not a food critic by any means. I like what I like and I tend not to be overly adventurous, but I was in New Mexico, I had flown for the first time ever and been totally lost in two airports. I had even used the bathroom on a plane while it was thirty thousand feet in the air. I was ready for anything. So when my friend took me out to eat at an authentic Mexican restaurant, I knew I would enjoy myself. I tried to order, but apparently my thick accent was too much and she had to order my meal. I had never been far enough away from my home that I was the one with an accent. Anyway she ordered and they asked green or red chili? I was feeling brave so I said green and they asked on top or on the side? I said on top and my friend said on the side with an order of bread. The waitress gave a knowing smile and walked away. I asked my friend what the big deal was and she explained that green chili was a bit spicy and I would probably not be able to handle it being on top of all my food. It is a common addition in New Mexico, but as it turns out not comparable to anything from my hometown. My meal finally arrived and a large bowl of steaming green chili was placed beside it. I do not know why but I was surprised that it was actually green. To prove a point I grabbed a large spoonful and dug in to the steamy bowl. The flavor hit my taste buds immediately and instead of being smart and spitting out the chili I swallowed. I felt like my mouth was on fire. I am someone who drinks hot chocolate cold and who thinks Doritos are too spicy, I thought I was dying. Apparently the waitress had watched this whole scene unfold and with her and my friend as well as many other diners laughing she brought me a glass of milk and some bread. That meal I learned that proving a point is not worth killing your taste buds and that though red is typically associated with hot, green should be too. Since that day I have tried green chili again, but only in small amounts with a great deal of bread and milk on standby.

THINGS I NEEDED TO SAY

ID: 472

It was a day like any other, but it was one that I enjoyed even more. I was over at my friend's house being all geeky and fan girl like with them. It had been quite a bit of time since I last goofed around, with the pressure of exams and all. Then my father arrived to pick me up, I said good bye to my friends and I'd see them in school. Like a stray bullet out of nowhere, the news finally reached my ears when I came home. My grandfather died that morning. My grandfather that would always just smile and try to laugh at my jokes even when they weren't funny. My grandfather that I saw just last week. Gone. Without a word, just leaving all loved ones behind. The shock lasted a long time for me, I just went into my room. I didn't cry yet. I would just be staring into the depths of my television set trying to think of something else. And then the sadness hit me. I was able to say good bye to my friends, but never to my grandfather. I never got to hug him. I never got to kiss him on the cheek. I never got to hold his hand. There were so many things I needed to say, so many things left unheard. I wanted to hear his stories about World War II, I was just too shy to ask. Yet, at this point in time I had yet to shed any tears. It was during the wake, when I saw his soul-less body that the tears gushed out of me. The only thing I could do then was whisper good bye to his body and hope that his soul was there and heard me say I love you and I'll miss you.

I LIKE KOO-KOO NUTS, DO YOU?

ID: 298

I was born and lived the first 9 years of my life on a land filled with coconuts, called Ben Tre in Vietnam. I loved drinking and eating the coconuts there. Then one day I moved to the US and there's absolutely no fresh coconut here. So whenever I go somewhere warm that grows coconut I always seek it out and drink as much as I can until my belly wants to burst. It's my obsession. I drank so much that one time the seller asked me, "are you trying to commit suicide?" lol.

Anyways, I recently went on a cruise. One of our stops was at Grand Cayman. Like usual I sought out coconuts and luckily there's one stand right outside the pier. The coconuts there were WICKED sweet, MUCH better than the ones found in Bahamas and Jamaica and maybe, just maybe, Hawaii. I had one when I first got off the pier, then I went to the bathroom, then I went out to play for hours. On my way back to the ship, I was going to drink only two, but after playing with the stingray and snorkeling for hours in the ocean I was tired, thirsty, and hungry so I ended up drinking and eating 5 coconuts total. I almost went for a 6th but mom wouldn't let me. She started trying to stop me after the second one, but I was stubborn and fought my way through the 5th one, but lost to her on the 6th one. I even tried convincing other tourists walking by to try the coconuts. The seller was so happy to get so much business from me and the tourists that he called me his Customer Of the Year. It's funny. So when I left with mom to get onto the ferry to go back to the cruise ship I wasn't perfectly happy because I didn't have my 6th coconut and that made me feel incomplete. It takes the ferry about 15 minutes to get to the cruise ship. About 5 minutes into the ride on the ferry, I felt like I needed to pee. Normally I can hold for a good half an hour to an hour no problem. But that day OH MY GOD, my bladder expanded so fast I thought I had no filter between my throat and the bladder. The last 10 minute ride back to the cruise ship was horrific. I had to pee so bad that I cut in front of an elder walking with a cane and sort of shoved him over to the side just so that I could get off the ferry quicker. He didn't complain but I still felt bad afterward. I got off the ferry, onto the cruise ship, and walked with my thighs together and my body bending in an awkward position all the way to the elevator. I got there looking miserable. Everyone was looking at me as if there's something wrong and that made me compel to tell the truth so I flat out said "I just gotta pee really bad." That was a mistake. A couple guys there started making the pee sound and people were sort of laughing at me all the way up to my floor. Before I got off the elevator one of the guys even said "enjoy!" The hallway on the cruise ship down to my room felt like 10 miles away, but I made it to the toilet just in time. I swear, I have never moaned in my life as loud as when I was peeing that day, even way louder than during any orgasm I ever had. The guy in the elevator was right, I did enjoy it! LOL.

The lesson here is to always drink moderately regardless how much you love a certain drink. If you're going to drink a lot, don't forget you'll need to pee, REALLY SOON and find a bathroom!

WHY WON'T YOU FLUSH!!!!!

ID: 45

As a child I had a problem, flushing toilets... Well I always ended up clogging the toilet, so one day I had clogged the toilet and didn't tell anyone. My dad ended up seeing that the toilet was clogged and he went to come ask my brother and I to see who had done it. I was afraid of what was going to happen, so I didn't admit to him that I had done it, instead I kept on whispering to my brother, while crying, to tell my dad that he had done it and not me. My brother, after several minutes, finally decided to take the blame. He had gotten into more trouble, than I did. To this day I still feel guilty. Lesson learned, always admit your faults when it comes to family.

My Lan T. Tran

WASH YOUR HANDS

ID: 326

I am not a germaphobe but I am generally quite careful with washing my hands. I was on the bus the other day and it was packed as usual. I was holding on to the metal railing for support. Without thinking about it, I rubbed my eye. Yikes. The next day I woke up and my eye was bloodshot and swollen. I had gotten an eye infection (not pinkeye, thank goodness) from rubbing my eye without washing my hands! So gross!

THE BLUES IS NOT FOR CHURCH

ID: 124

I started taking piano lessons when I was about eight years old. I loved playing the piano and for years had played by ear, but my mother finally decided on formal lessons. My piano teacher was great and she quickly taught me to read music and play chords. I moved through the books quickly, but like most kids, hated practicing. My mother had wanted me to learn to play for church, but I hated the slow drawn out hymns that filled the books. My piano teacher did not want me to lose my love of music so she taught me a very simple, but very fast song she called the Louisiana Blues. I loved the song and practiced it every day so that I could play it as fast as possible and still sound good. I also practiced my other music, but it was by far my favorite. One week before church I was sitting in the sanctuary practicing for the service when the urge to play my favorite song hit. No one was around so I slammed out the first notes and took off from there. That old Baptist piano had probably never heard or felt such music. Just as I was finishing up with a large smile on my face, I looked up to see most of the congregation staring at me wide mouthed. My smile faded and the pastor leaned down and whispered to me that the blues was not church appropriate. I am now 20 years older and that is the one thing my grandmother remembers about my years of playing at the church. I guess my lesson was that if you are going to play the blues at church, you should make sure the sanctuary doors are locked.

Mistakes In Life: The Path To Wisdom

TRAGEDY IS THE MOTHER OF NECESSITY

ID: 504

This happened when the company I worked was retrenching; I was one of those employees who were retrenched; so I was jobless and helpless. I didn't want to go back to my hometown jobless because I didn't want to be a burden to my parents. There was this guy who was more than willing to take care of me as long as I would be willing to live with him. Since I was so helpless at that time, I went with him without even thinking the consequences.

It took me a long time to adjust, since I never knew him that well, not to mention that I never felt anything for him; I just lived with him since I had nowhere to go. As expected after two years of living with him, I got pregnant. This time I promised myself I would never do what I had done in my previous marriage. I would be docile and learn to serve him well this time; which I truly did.

I thought that by being submissive, I would never have a problem with my relationship. However, my life was even more miserable; good thing, I always caught him because of this new technology. One day he got home very late, told me that they were having an overtime which I pretended to believe. When he fell asleep I took his cell phone and read all the messages. Well, I was not surprised to see the messages of the girl he was dating that night. I was so mad that I was not able to control myself.

Even when he was sleeping I slapped him and beat him hard. We had a fierce fight; and even though I was pregnant, I left him in the middle of the night. All of my fury during the time I caught my husband womanizing came back to me. I said to myself that all men are the same, philanderers, womanizers and unfaithful. I went to my friend's house and stayed there for a while.

I thought that the incident would be the last but it happened not just once, but many times. My life was in complete misery until I arrived at a point where enough was enough. I made him choose between his boss and myself; since it was his boss who always took him bar hopping and night clubbing every night. I told him that if he chose me then he must quit his job, but if he chose his boss then he could never see me and his son.

To make the story short, he chose me; thus both of us are jobless with a son to feed. I told him that we must start a new life together and find a way to solve our financial adversity.

Lesson: When getting into a serious relationship, you must never commit to anyone you never knew so well, otherwise you will end up miserable.

LOST PHONE

ID: 61

When mobile phones were first introduced to the market, I was so eager to own one for myself. When I got my first paycheck, I bought one for myself and I was very happy with it. One day I was on a bus going to town to meet my dad, and because he also had a phone, I told him I would call him and let him know where we would meet. While on the bus, I sat next to a man who was busy reading the newspaper. What I didn't know was that he was a thief and he was just using the newspaper as a cover for his evil plans. Without my knowledge, he opened my bag, took my phone, and immediately got off the bus. When I got to town, I looked for my phone in order to call my dad, but the phone was nowhere to be found. I immediately concluded that the man had removed it from my bag. My dad tried to call my phone, but it went unanswered and later it was switched off. I was so heartbroken that from that day on, I learned to hold my things tightly even when I am on a bus. Always be cautious of the person you sit next to.

Mistakes In Life: The Path To Wisdom

TO GO NATURAL OR NOT

ID: 356

After hearing of all of the health problems associated with antiperspirant, I bravely decided to go for a natural deodorant instead. This is fine on most days although I still sweat a little bit. Oral exams are a different story. I had an exam a few weeks ago and wore the natural deodorant. I also wore a thin blue shirt. I was so nervous that I sweat right through that shirt and had lovely wet spots underneath my arms. SO embarrassing! While I still want to be healthy and wear my natural deodorant, I think I will keep some of the strong stuff on hand for these kinds of situations.

BUT IT LIVES IN THE SNOW

ID: 163

We moved a couple of years ago to a state that gets much more snow than we are used to getting. So after the first seven or eight inches fell overnight it was decided that we must buy a snow shovel for the driveway and walk. So out we went to buy a snow shovel, we were prepared for the next big snow storm. About a week later that snow storm happened and I was so happy that I could shovel a path for my car to leave the garage this time. I wrapped myself in layers of clothing and headed out to grab the shovel, but it was nowhere to be found. I asked my better half who had not seen it and then started to question the kids. I have found when things go missing they often have something to do with it. Everyone denied knowing where the new shovel had gotten to. I was angry, but I undressed and went back in until I could borrow a shovel from a neighbor. About an hour later my youngest came downstairs with that I'm sorry look painted on his face. He climbed on my lap and said, "Mommy the shovel is where he lives." I just looked at him confused and asked what he meant. "The snow shovel lives in the snow." That's when it hit me. "Sweetie, did you put the shovel outside so it could live in the snow?" "Yes". "When did you do that?" "Two days ago." My heart sank because if the snow shovel had been out for two days then it was under about ten inches of snow. I asked if he knew where he put the shovel and he said he did. The whole family spent an hour looking for a buried snow shovel. We all went in with frozen noses and no shovel. It was an exceptionally bad winter and we, unfortunately, did not see the shovel until spring. Now the shovels are all kept in a locked closet in the garage and my youngest has learned that even though the name suggests otherwise, snow shovels live in the garage.

GRAB THE OPPORTUNITY
ID: 540

My biggest regret in life was when I got hired in a call center. I was about to have training for three weeks, but I decided not to take the job. I was a fresh college graduate and all I wanted to do was to enjoy my first my summer, which was why I did not grab the job. I thought there would be another job opportunity for me. After summer I decided to find a job. I passed in an application letter to every hiring company but none of them called me for an interview. So here I am now, I'm still jobless. In life opportunity knocks once, that's why we need to grab it while it's there, because we don't know if there will be an opportunity like that again.

SHARPIES ARE NOT FACE PAINT
ID: 81

When my daughter was very young, she developed a love of art. She was constantly drawing and paper and crayons were never in short supply at our home. Once her brother was born, she tried her hardest to get him to draw and color with her, but he was not interested. When they were 4 and 2 and I was pregnant with number three, we went to a county fair. The fair had a face painting booth that quickly caught the attention of my daughter. She wanted a butterfly on her face so we gave in and had it painted. She wore her butterfly mask proudly and told everyone that would listen that she was the queen butterfly. That night she would not let me wash it off and knowing that it would rub off that night I put on an old sheet and pillowcase and let her sleep as queen butterfly. The next morning she was

Mistakes In Life: The Path To Wisdom

so upset that the paint had worn off, but I promised her we would buy some face paint soon and I would paint her face again.

Well time went on and we did buy face paint and for weeks she had new little designs on her face. She loved looking at herself in the mirror and taking on the personality of whatever happened to be painted on her face. Once the face paint ran out I also thought the obsession ran out, but I was proven wrong less than a week later. As it turns out, she had decided to become the painter which I discovered one morning when I went to get them up for breakfast. I walked into her room and was sweetly surprised to find her little brother asleep with her in the bed. They looked so cute lying there sound asleep, that is until I picked up my cute little two year old who had had tiger stripes painted all over his face. The worst part was that she had not used paint or even regular markers; instead she had used Sharpies, permanent markers. My poor little boy was a tiger for almost a week before all the stripes could be scrubbed off. My daughter had once again taught me a lesson, well two. One, always keep the Sharpies on a high shelf and two, let nothing surprise you with children.

NEVER FOLLOW THE CROWD

ID: 390

When I started college, I was hanging out with some people who smoked cigarettes. I had never smoked all through high school, and was not really interested. I decided that it was ok to smoke "socially" having one every once in a while, because I wasn't addicted and it was not a big deal. Eventually I started realizing that I WAS becoming addicted, and was buying them myself. A few years later I still smoke, and sincerely wish I had never started smoking, even socially. No one ever pressured me; it was just that I thought it was no big deal. And now I'm stuck addicted to cigarettes, it is a big deal. Quitting is hard, and I learned that it is definitely not worth it just to be a part of the crowd.

My Lan T. Tran

MY SECOND CHANCE

ID: 561

Growing up wasn't easy for me. When I was young, I felt special and loved but as time went by; I grew to become a rebellious teenager. Mistakes had become quite common for me during that time and despite the constant reminders from my parents, I never listened. Probably one of the biggest mistakes that I had made in the past was when I was in college. It was my first year then. I had a steady boyfriend then and my parents lived in another country so I was pretty much alone. Forced to become more independent, I needed to follow my sense of judgment in almost everything. I felt empowered but at the same, intimidated by the responsibility bestowed upon me. I knew I had to study hard to make my parents proud but somehow when I was there, I just couldn't.

One of the biggest distractions to me during that time was my then boyfriend. He always asked me out on dates. He was in the same boat as I was. He felt lonely and he knew I would understand him, knowing that I was also experiencing the same thing. Because we spent most of our time together, we neglected many other things. We forgot our social lives, our duties and responsibilities, our dreams and promises and most of all, our studies. It was my second year in college when I realized that things were getting out of hand. As I enrolled for my classes, I saw my grades flash before me. The comments that my teachers have given me were not all good. I was slipping and there wasn't anything I could do. I struggled to stay in the condition that I was in. I was desperate to get back on track. As I continued to do so, I explained the situation to my boyfriend who back then was also having the same dilemma as I. We were both screwed and knew we had to inform our parents somehow someway. We were scared and we knew it was both our fault for slacking and not taking our studies seriously. That night, I confessed everything to them about what had happened to me during the past year. It was difficult for them to understand. They blamed me for what happened. I felt horrible after that. Unfortunately, the reaction I was expecting wasn't just that. I thought that they would somehow continue to encourage me to try harder despite everything that had happened but they did not.

Later that year, I dropped out of college. My parents and I drifted after that and I broke up with my boyfriend. I became a loner after everything that had happened. I didn't want to face the world anymore. I thought that maybe ending my existence was the only way to help me end my misery. After overdosing myself with pills, I lay down in my bed and closed my eyes, waiting for death to come to me. I woke up in the afternoon the next day with a throbbing headache. I did not die the night before. I was still in one piece. Suddenly, it was like my life flashed before me. I felt guilty for ever thinking of ending myself. That day, I learned to become stronger. After a few months of trying to get up on my own feet once again, I was ready to repair my relationship with my parents. They were no longer angry with me and after seeing what I had become and what I had gone through, they realized that I needed redemption. I asked for a second chance and was given one. I am proud to say that my ordeal made me learn so many things. I learned that parents will always be there for you no matter what and that it is never too late to pick yourself up and try again. I feel like I am living a second life and I couldn't be more thankful to those who trusted in me once more.

INSOMNIA ATTACK!

ID: 241

I suffered from a couple cases of terrible insomnia a few years ago. One of my friends had the same problem too, and we both agreed that sleeplessness at night is not only due to the food intake or what you drink during the day (especially too many cups of coffee). But I have to say, it's also because of some bad habits. When I was younger, I was really active. In fact, I was an athlete at some point. However, when I reached a university, that's when I had started having trouble with sleeping at night. I always stayed up late every night. Then this habit took a toll on me; I was lethargic during the day, snacked a lot, was always irritable, developed acne, and had really dry skin. This went on until I started working and met a colleague who had said to me she had the same thing – sleeping problems. She tried a lot of things to get back to a proper bedtime, like nine o'clock at night. At first, she said it was quite frustrating just lying in bed and stressing herself out to sleep. Then she went to making sort of her own remedy. In the morning, she would wake up as usual, get into some active workout, and try to avoid sitting down at break time in the office. Also she made a mixture of honey and milk which she drank an hour prior to hitting the sack. And before she even realized it, she was already changing an old pattern into a 'new' and more healthful habit. I tried it for myself and I must say it also worked for me! From then on, I think my skin has gone back to normal. And today I feel more energetic and I like the fact that I can sleep much better now than ever before.

CHOOSE POSITIVE PEOPLE TO INFLUENCE YOURSELF

ID: 433

While I enjoy having a different group of people to be my friends, whether they have different values or personalities from my own, I think in the end, we gravitate towards the people that best reflect our own inner beliefs and self. I used to hang with people that were lacking in basic morals. But then of course, being a true friend I never passed judgment to them since I firmly believe that we are fighting our own battles. But over the years, having them around seemed more like a burden to me because we always clashed in terms of our ideals in life. While they went on with their lives trying to drag me into their kind of lifestyle, opposing mine, I realized it was time to move on. I met a colleague that once said to me, you cannot choose your relatives but you can choose friends, so why not choose the ones that will influence you in the most positive way? I tried to change my outlook towards life, not entirely in a religious sense, but more of being true to what I felt inside. In the past where I used to just smile even though my friends would verbally abuse me, now I just walk away and put a stop to all the abuse. I don't think I need people that cuss me, talking me down because I was slow in deciding, or taunting me because I was too shy or conservative to chase a boy. In the real world, it is considered emotional manipulation and it is only sad I did not make the choice earlier to recognize it and cut the friendship. I learned that as I became more positive about myself, the more I tended to move towards people that shared my ideals, are encouraging more than imposing, and more gentle rather than pushy. And I have made the right decision in choosing the positive thinkers and let them influence me this way.

Mistakes In Life: The Path To Wisdom

MONEY IS NOT EVERYTHING

ID: 584

Once I thought money was everything, money could do anything. That's why I was chasing it. Money was my only concern at that time. Nothing else could make me happy, except money. I was careless about everything else.

I succeeded in business, earned a lot of money. But I did not get any peace. Rather I was at a far distance from everyone close to me. My life turned into hell. Although I had a lot of money, I could not use it to make my life better. It turned worse day by day, but I could not help myself.

Until I realized, money is not everything. Money can give us wealth and power, but cannot give us peace. And everyone needs peace and happiness, not power. So stop chasing money or it will ruin your peace and all the happiness.

OBEDIENCE

ID: 20

When I was growing up, my parents would assign chores to my siblings and I and they would supervise if the duties were performed as per their instructions. One day they assigned duties and went away. Because we knew they would be away the entire day, we decided to play first and attend to our duties later, only for them to return earlier than we expected. Because we could see them from a distance, we ran and rushed our duties. Because I was supposed to wash the utensils, I did it so poorly that my mom discovered they were not properly cleaned. She then realized that I had just done it hastily. She was so sure we had spent the whole day playing because most of the assignments had not been done. At that point I was given a beating that taught me to obey. From that time on, I finished my duties before playing with other children.

My Lan T. Tran

WHEN "DON'T SWEAT THE SMALL STUFF" ISN'T TRUE

ID: 104

I once worked as an assistant to one of the sales manager of a famous software company. The company built a satellite office in Asia where I was assigned. My boss, the sales manager, was a very enthusiastic person, was very good with people, and an expert at his skill – SALES. During the first year that the office was in operation, we hit and even exceeded our sales targets for up to 280%. We were very happy, rich, and popular with the other Sales teams amongst the whole business. The start of the fiscal year that followed turned out to be easy too. By May, we had around 10 prospects in the pipeline, which was going to be hard work because we only usually deal with one to three at a time. At this point, we knew we could not work on all 10, so we said, we just choose the most feasible projects to work on. I was inclined to choose the smaller ones, as they were easier to work on, and you get points for popularity if the deal is closed for all three. My colleague on the other hand, wanted to get the biggest account, so he said we just have to go through one hardship. Being just his assistant, I gave in – I supported him even if deep inside I was not feeling good about it. He even told me not to waste my time on these small accounts. After several months of hard work through the sales cycle, guess what – we came out empty handed. By this time, we had already given out all other nine accounts to the other teams and going back to them was no longer possible because the other teams have already CLOSED THE SALE, in two months after we gave it to them! Our end of year was literally ZERO. I felt so bad that I wanted to vent my frustration via Facebook. After reading through articles about missing sales opportunities, I came across this very applicable quote, by Hugh Allen: Jumping at several small opportunities may get us there more quickly than waiting for one big one to come along.

LESSON FROM ENVIOUSNESS

ID: 474

It is always bad to envy someone or get jealous from seeing someone flourishing. But this is common nature for a human being to get envious by seeing others prosper. I do it too. I was a boy of 17 years at that time. I used to envy my brother who was also my age but not from my status in terms of his family and educational experiences. He dropped out of the educational system at a very young age because of some family problems. I used to compare my success with his and showed everyone in my family how successful I was in terms of him. Everyone also praised me. But now, 9 years later, he has a very good job in his career. He now earns more than $500 per month by using all his professional and real life experiences, whereas I am still a student who is thirsting for a degree. Sometimes I feel that I might need his help to get an Internship in the company he is working for. Everyone in my family also thundered with his dramatic exposure and income level and felt upset with me because I am still not earning money for my family. From that day on, I understood that I should never envy or degrade anyone because one day you might need them.

SAYING NO – MAKING IT A HABIT

ID: 302

As a person with a very low self-esteem, I always tried to please friends and would get really anxious if I let someone down. Back when I was in school, many of my classmates and friends with whom I used to share a house would pass on tasks to me, knowing I never said no. And I would show how happy I was doing favors for them. One day, I hit rock-bottom broke and had not a single penny left in my purse. I expected a few friends whom I helped with their thesis papers pro bono, to also help me out, but alas, no one really came. It made me very sad and quite disappointed with my own naive expectations. As I grew more mature, I learned that most of the things which stressed me out came from my own actions, one of which was saying yes to pretty much everything and everyone in an effort to save them some disappointment. I read self-help materials and books which encouraged building one's self-confidence as well as keeping a positive attitude towards life. One of my favorite lines is from someone famous who said, "It's okay to say no", which I applied to my life. I think in a lot of ways, this approach has improved the way I see myself when I deal with people. I have learned that it is not the other person's fault if they could not reach out to you in times of trouble. My expectations are my own disappointments and I have to learn to deal with them for the rest of my life. What I need to focus on more now is improving myself so I can be a more confident and positive person who can be there for others when they need me.

BROKEN RELATIONSHIP

ID: 46

I met Mr. Right on campus who was a year ahead of me when I was in my second year in college. Our relationship thrived and it was the talk of the entire campus because people envied us on how we related. The relationship matured and I believed that this was my prince that I would spend the rest of my life with. The guy completed his degree and he got a job and I thought I was one of the few lucky girls but I was wrong. They say you can only know a person well after they get money and for sure they are right, because this guy changed and started dating many other girls who were working. I also finished my course and got a job and one day when I was on leave I decided to pay him a surprise visit only to find him with another girl in the house. I was so heartbroken and I thought that was the end of my life because I had been in that relationship for over 6 years and I had introduced him to my parents, relatives and friends. He had likewise introduced me and we were in the process of planning for a wedding. I thought walking away would be the worst thing to ever happen to me but over the years I now appreciate having walked away from a relationship that was full of unfaithfulness. I met another man who married me and we are now happily married. I learned that it is better to walk away from a relationship than to break a marriage. My word of advice is that if you are not happy in a relationship don't think you will be happy in a marriage with that partner. Stop hanging on a relationship that is causing heartache. You are precious and there is a better person for you out there.

Mistakes In Life: The Path To Wisdom

CRACKING ELBOW

ID: 330

I have a bad habit of cracking my knuckles from my fingers to my neck to my feet every day. One day my right elbow felt a little weird so I cracked it like I normally do when it's not hurting thinking that will get rid of it. It got a little worse after that, but still not bad enough for me to pay attention. Then the next day I went grocery shopping and carried lots of heavy bags. I didn't think it was a big deal carrying it with my right arm even though I did feel the pain, but it turned out to be a big deal. My elbow hurt pretty bad after that. It's been more than two weeks and it's still hurting. The lesson learned is to pay attention to any body part that's hurting even though it seems minor. Minor pain can turn into major pain if not taken care of right away, especially when you're older.

WANT TO VOLUNTEER? THINK AGAIN

ID: 126

Being the eldest in the family, I have always been the "dependable one," the "reliable one," everybody's "jane-of-all-trades." I never complained until now. I just realized that doing things for the family is indeed satisfying, it gives me a different feeling about commitment, but it also buries me down into a lot of workload.

Just recently, my mom and my aunt purchased a condo unit each and because those units are in the same city where I work, I (almost) screamed "ME! ME! ME!" s as soon as I heard them say "I wonder who can get these documents processed."

A month later I am now stuck between sending documents to and fro, paying this and that, and worse, I am now being blamed for whatever delay is being experienced with the paperwork. I have been sick for almost a month but nobody seemed to have remembered that as a cause for the delay. I'm now getting calls from everywhere in relation to these documents. I'm even spending my own money to get these things done.

My Lan T. Tran

I so regret being such a "good and dependable daughter" in this perspective. I vow that from now on, no more "pro-bono" volunteer work.

MISTAKES FROM MY IMMATURITY
ID: 505

When I was a boy of 16 I used to be very wicked. I bet with my friends over any issue. I went with them for smoking and engaged myself in many bad habits. I got addicted to my friends so much that sometimes I had to steal money from my home to meet my friend's expectations. Often my friend would ask me for money referring to themselves as very poor, they even cried before me. I was too affectionate to them and even felt weak towards them. Because of my bad habits, I could not deny them. But I denied my parents' hard work and their money. One day I found that my friends were not that poor to take money from them. One of my friends told me that everyone has some bad habits of course but never they spoil their own money for this. Your parent's money is your own. Stealing from them means you are stealing from your own pocket. His words shook my mind and I decided to skip all my bad habits with my parent's money. If there's anytime I can manage on my own then I will fulfill my desires.

EATING THE DEITY'S CANDY
ID: 62

When I first moved to Asia, I was working for a school that catered to students from all over Asia.

On my second day of work, I noticed there was a bowl full of candy on a table in the reception area which I thought was meant for guests of the school, such as parents, etc. So as I passed by the reception, I helped myself to piece of candy and gave a friendly 'hello' to the people in the room, who seemed to be a bunch of parents just about to have a tour of the school.

When I returned to the reception area a few moments later, I saw that there was a huge Buddha statue next to the candy, and then it hit me... the candy was supposed to be an offering for the Buddha. At that point I also realized that the whole group of people were now sending a bunch of disapproving looks in my direction.

I check twice before taking 'free' candy now.

LOVE AT 18

ID: 359

"Love" as you experience it when you're 18 years old is not as real as you think it is. During my freshman year in college I fell in love with a classmate. I defied all odds to be with him, especially since our religions were different. My father was against our relationship and even threatened to have me quit school. I was rebellious and defied them every step of the way. I stopped attending my classes and decided to work in the meantime.

I thought that true love requires sacrifice and that my parents did not seem to understand how serious we were in our relationship. This situation wore on for three months, until my then-boyfriend informed me that since his parents would stop supporting him financially he decided to break-up with me, he could not bear parting with his monthly allowance. I was heartbroken; I then realized that I was the only one who thought that our relationship would defy all odds. But then I was too young.

After having been in a few relationships, I can easily say that a mature relationship requires a couple to understand what it means to be there for each other and to have a common outlook in life. Love does not only mean "feeling love" but rather it entails being committed and supporting each other when faced with life's circumstances.

My Lan T. Tran

DON'T SLEEP IN THE BUS, EPISODE 2
ID: 165

After Episode 1 of my do-not-sleep-in-the-bus story, the careless act of me sleeping happened yet again. Still with my first job, but this time around a year later, I fell asleep again.

On my way home after the graveyard shift, I got on the bus and approached the rear section, wanting to sit comfortably without any seatmates. (People prefer to sit in the front so it would be easier for them to get off.) The place I now live at is convenient – I get off at the bus terminal and then get another ride towards home. I guess I was really tired that day... again, I don't remember anything from the time I paid my fare until I got off – at the wrong place this time!

I don't know how much time had passed, but I fell into panic mode when, as I woke up, I was in an unfamiliar place. I checked my watch, it had been three hours since I boarded! I was also alone in the bus now so I immediately got up and approached the front, and then the bus driver was surprised to see me. He told me "I'm going to somewhere else now, dear. Did you fall asleep?" My heart jumped! I didn't know the place, and so I told him I needed to get off. He gave me instructions on how to go back to the terminal.

I felt relieved but really annoyed at the same time. All I could think of was: oh-my-god-I-fell-asleep-again. I should have been home two hours ago. I guess it is really stupid committing the same mistake twice, but now I have become more vigilant. I am now more conscious of what I do, especially on the bus. From seven years ago until now, the sleeping-in-the-bus incident has never happened again.

DON'T JUST FOLLOW THE HEART
ID: 545

When I was just starting with my career, I got invited by a couple of officemates to go for drinks at the end of the day. I thought, "Oh yeah, that would be fun but I really have a huge deadline to meet tomorrow morning and I have not accomplished a lot." Despite the inhibitions, I still joined my friends and partied all night. It was definitely fun, but when I got home it was like I came from a fantasy world and now I was back to reality. I was doomed. There was no way I could have finished the things I should have done in just a little time. I worked my way to finishing everything even if it was not that excellent. I finished the project on time but not how I planned it to be. Good thing I got away with the consequences that time, but in the next occasion what happens? So, I realized that when we follow our hearts, yes it would make us happy but will happiness last for long? Somehow you will fall. So, weigh everything you decide on. Think hard. Would it be responsible to do that? Would that be creating a good image of you? Stop and think twice.

LOW SELF ESTEEM

ID: 84

Many years ago, I thought I was the most insecure person I had ever known. I didn't have any confidence in myself or in anything I did. I always compared myself to other people. The way I dressed, the way I spoke and acted should always conform to what was acceptable to many. If I saw that one of my classmates had a new bag, I would then ask my parents to buy me a new one. If a new style of dress was the new trend in our school, I would instantly whine to my parents that I needed that new dress. I was just lucky enough to have generous parents. However, this did not help my self-esteem. Every time there was a new popular girl in school, I couldn't help but compare myself to her; I asked myself if I was prettier or why the guys and my classmates liked her. I would end up competing against that person and bullying her with my friends. Then I found out that even the people I knew were not happy with the person I became. They thought that being with me made them feel like they were inadequate. That they needed to always upgrade themselves to consider themselves my friends. That they cannot be themselves around me. I felt that they seemed distant to me and that I couldn't tell them what I was really feeling anymore. In the end I ended up losing their true friendship and most of all losing my self-confidence.

My Lan T. Tran

I only gained my self-esteem back when we moved to a different city because of my mom's job. I had changed my point of view and values. I didn't compare myself anymore to anyone. Because I realized, there is always someone who is better than me. I had understood that whenever I compare myself to someone who is prettier or smarter than me, it will only make me feel bad and little about myself. I now make it a point to count the things that I have improved on and have achieved. I am more confident now of myself and the things I can do. I know that I am unique and beautiful in my own way.

PUPPIES ARE HARD WORK
ID: 392

A few months ago I was looking for a gift for my stepfather, because his dog had passed away and he was looking for a new one. My sister and I had looked all over and found puppies. My stepdad was very excited about the gift, but after a little bit, his health took a turn for the worse and he wasn't able to take care of them. I had to take them with me for a while. It was pretty difficult for me to find homes for them, and during the time that they lived with me it was very very hard to train them, and teach them right from wrong. I learned a lot from the short time that they lived with me, as I had never raised puppies before. I learned responsibility, and patience, both very important things to have when trying to take care of little baby puppies.

A LESSON IN PRIDE
ID: 205

When I was 14 I was very self-conscious (as many teens are). When I fell hard in floor hockey I knew I had damaged something but didn't want to go to the doctor, for fear that he would have to see me naked. 15 years later I am having trouble sitting and going to the bathroom. I finally sucked up my pride and my doctor sent me for an x-ray. I had been living with a broken tailbone for all of these years, which had fused in a crooked position and was causing a lot of pain. Now I feel ashamed that I had left it for so long. The positioning of my tailbone does not allow me to have a natural childbirth. If I had gone to the doctor when I first got injured, I could have possibly prevented years of pain, as well as the difficult reality that I will not be able to deliver a child without a C-section.

The take away message is: swallow your pride! Especially you men – don't ignore your body when it tells you something is wrong!

FUN AND A BROKEN BONE

ID: 495

I was just 8 years old at the time when I was told not to go out of the house. I was just a normal boy living a very simple life. I really love to go out and play with other kids outside the house. They would always call for me to go out and play hide and seek, tag games and any other games a child would want to play with other children. My mom was a business woman. She never had time to look after me because every day, she would wake up early at 7am for work and come home at 7pm; she was always tired after coming home. My dad died when I was just 4 years old. Every day it would be my nanny and me who were left inside the house. One sunny afternoon, two of my closest friends called me to go biking at the park. Good thing was that my nanny was sleeping. I silently sneaked outside the house and climbed over our gate just to get out. I was so happy that I made it outside without my nanny noticing I had snuck out. One of my friends, Junil, loaned me his bike as he rode over at the back of the bike of Pagong, my second friend. The three of us together went to the park to get some fresh air and to stroll around with our bicycles. The park was 3 kilometers away from our house and for us that was a bit far. I was riding the bike as fast as I could around the park. It was so nice that the air I felt made me feel like I was flying as I picked up speed. Suddenly out of nowhere, Junil appeared 10 meters in front of me. I never noticed him coming right at me. He was even smiling. He knew which way to turn as he picked up speed. I was surprised and did not know what to do as I watched him closing in. At the moment we came within touching distance of each other, he turned to the right while I was afraid and nervous. I turned to the left and in just a blink of an eye we crashed; I woke up lying on the road with the bikes over our bodies. We laughed as I tried to get up knowing that we were okay but, my whole body felt weak like I didn't have the energy to stand up. As I desperately stood up, I tried lifting the bicycle and suddenly I felt a snap on my right shoulder. It was broken and it was the worst pain I had ever felt at that time. It was like there was blood gushing from the inside of my shoulder as I tried to move and slowly walk under the shade of a tree. I told my friends to go home without me and to call my mom to fetch me at the park. The bike I was riding was severely damaged and it was a good thing I did not hit my head. 30 minutes later, my mom came and drove me to the nearest hospital. She had to leave the shop to take care of me the whole day. After that, I was scolded and grounded for a month and my mom had to pay for the broken bicycle and she fired the nanny; poor nanny never knew what was coming. Accidents can and will happen and will hit you without you knowing it. It happens for no reason at all. So take care always and keep an eye on the road! I love my mom and always will. Love your mom because they are the best thing in the world!

SAFETY IN THE BATHROOM

ID: 245

I was rushing to get to a meeting and hurriedly dashed into the washroom to get all my business done. As I was about to step into the shower, I didn't realize that one of my children's toys was lying around. I accidentally stepped on it, lost my balance, and had an awkward fall on my backside. Fortunately enough for me, it wasn't too hard a fall, since I was able to cling on to the shower curtains which got ripped in the process. It sort of minimized the accident, although my backside hurt for a while. I called my husband and he tried to help me up and checked if I was ok. I said I was fine and all, and gladly made it to the meeting with only a very minimal sort of shuffle and a tiny concussion. When I got home, my husband and I made a house rule never to leave toys or potentially harmful objects lying anywhere in the house. We explained to the children that any kind of toy that rolls or has wheels can puncture or hurt one of us in the house and these must be kept away. I'm so glad to have nice kids – they have agreed to it and sworn to keep their promise. Now we have a safer home with well-informed children.

ADVICE FROM A TEACHER

ID: 438

Years ago, I didn't believe in love. It was only a game for me. All I had in mind was, "Why waste my time on one girl, when I could have another"?

It all started when I was in secondary school, when I had a big crush on a girl. For years, I didn't have the guts to tell her how I felt. Then one day, I took all the courage I had, and blurted it all out to her. I was so happy when she became my very first girlfriend, but I turned out to be so wrong. I did all her assignments, I treated her every day. I was being used. I was so mad, that I promised myself that one day, I would get my revenge.

"College", I once said, "finally, I can have my revenge." I dated so many girls, either to get laid, or just for fun. I broke so many girls' hearts. One day, I met a girl who would soon change everything. She was pretty, intelligent, and sweet. I wanted to break that girl's heart, but days and weeks passed, I began to like her. I continued to date her, almost every single day. The anger in my heart slowly faded away, thanks to this girl.

Never be afraid to fall in love. Revenge is exactly the wrong thing to do. Pain, though how much painful it is, is all part of being in love. We learn and grow from it.

GET TOGETHER UNVEILS SECRETS

ID: 585

High school was the time in my life that had most ups and down but I still had good friends through the thick and thin situations. It is with this that a friend of mine, Anna, and I thought it would be good to get our friends to go for a hangout together and relive the good old days. Those who could make it were few but all the same, we were happy to see each other and catch up where we had left off and remembering the insane times we had at boarding school.

A restaurant was picked for this and food was in plenty. The laughter that filled the air was to envy as other customers looked on wondering what we were so happy about. It was then with the reminiscing that secrets started spilling one by one. Secrets of behind the scenes relationships of who did what with whose boyfriend back then started to spill.

There was so much disaster after that, that the management of the restaurant had to throw some of my friends out. It was an embarrassing situation that has made me to this day not to go back to that restaurant as I believe they would remember me by the incident.

The lesson from this was that in as much as you have common ground with people, the differences between them can be far and wide. Trying to relive the moments we had was not possible. The past is in the past and we can only look back and reminisce but cannot change it.

MISSING 60?

ID: 23

When I was about 8 or 9 years old, all I had on my mind was money. I would take out family member's purses and wallets just to count how much money they had. One day, I was walking around the house and I saw my cousin's coin tub. I looked inside, took out the tub, dumped all the money and started counting until I got to the bottom of the tub, and found $60, my mom called me to go home, I then put the $60 in my pocket. Later that day my uncle had called me questioning me about the money. I then out of fear had lied saying I didn't know anything and I didn't take anything. My mom had then asked me what happened I told her that my uncle thought I stole $60, my mom immediately knew I was lying, and told me to give her the money. I was then grounded for a while. The lesson here is whatever isn't yours don't touch, or take, or you will get penalized.

Mistakes In Life: The Path To Wisdom

CHECK THE ITEMS AGAINST THE RECEIPT

ID: 105

I had an unforgettable moment while grocery shopping. I usually don't pay much attention when the cashier punches my grocery items on the cash register. There was one time when I had a feeling that I had paid too much for the groceries. When the cashier told me the amount I just straightaway paid for it without even checking the receipt. When I got home, I couldn't get rid of the idea that there was something wrong with the price that I paid for all the items. So I checked all the items against the receipt and alas, I had found out that one of the items had been punched three times. As a result, I paid three times for that single item. Next thing, I found myself back in the grocery store, complaining about the error on my receipt and asking for a refund. It took much of my day just to correct a mistake that I could have prevented if I had been more attentive in the first place. From that day on, when I'm grocery shopping or buying anything, I always check every item punched on the cash register. I always check the receipt and make sure all the items are correctly entered before I leave the store. It may take a little more time and effort doing it, but it sure saves me a lot of trouble later.

CRYING OVER SPILT MILK

ID: 475

This experience is quite embarrassing, but somehow I wish readers would find a lesson from this.

Being the eldest in the family of five, I would say that I am the most favored child; although, all of us studied in private schools from our elementary days until college. When I was in college, I kept on shifting courses because my father chose engineering for me, which I never liked. Nevertheless, I took up engineering for three years, but because it was not my field I shifted to accountancy, which I never stayed in for long. I decided to quit, because I was uncertain what kind of degree would I pursue.

My Lan T. Tran

I took up Library Science when I went back to school. One day our dean announced that, CHED, would give a qualifying exam and those who emerge as the top 20 would be the official CHED scholars. Because of that, all of my friends were taking the exam; so, I took the exam as well. After a week, our guidance counselor called me, I was so anxious when I went into his office. My anxiety vanished, when he said "Congratulations you made it to the top, you got the third place!"

I was overwhelmed, but the message did not sink in yet. I felt nothing and thought nothing of that incident until the list of the top 10 examinees was posted on our campus bulletin board. After a week, all of the scholars were called for the orientation. We were told that the courses CHED would sponsor were BSED-English, Math, Biology, Physics, Chemistry, and Filipino. Anything other than those they would not support. Because of the privilege and benefits from the said scholarship I shifted again. I said that this time it would be for real.

Indeed, it was for real. I graduated in college with a BSED-Math. After graduation I took the review for the teacher's board exam and studied every day; but on the day of the board exam, I was not able to take it. I woke up late because I went bar hopping with my friends until the wee hours of the morning. When I woke up nobody was there in the hotel room, but myself; so, I slowly got my stuff and went home.

My father was extremely furious upon knowing what I had done. He told me that he would never spend a single cent for my board exam. And true to his word, he never supported me no matter how I asked for his help. I am really on my own now. During the release of the board exam result, the only name that was not on the bulletin board was mine. I felt so embarrassed, frustrated and disappointed; but it gave me a lesson though.

Lesson: Do not betray the trust that someone bestows on you. If you do, nobody will trust you anymore.

Mistakes In Life: The Path To Wisdom

NO BEANS ON YOUR FIRST DATE

ID: 304

My very first serious boyfriend in high school took me on our first date to see Romeo and Juliet the movie. I was rather uncomfortable on the date, as I am lactose intolerant and had cheese pasta for dinner. As he dropped me off at home, we both leaned in for our first kiss. This should have been romantic, but as I leaned in a fart slipped out. It was loud enough so he could hear it and I couldn't even pretend that it didn't happen. I tried to laugh it off and luckily he did too. Believe it or not, we continued dating for another year and a half. Ladies: when you are prepping for that big date, forego the beans (or dairy if you are like me)!

TELLING LIES

ID: 47

Whenever I see a river flowing, I remember the good old days when we used to fetch the water from the river because that is where I learned my first swimming lessons. Along with my other siblings and neighbors' kids, I would go to fetch water and take a swim, something that was prohibited by our parents because they feared that we would drown. Whenever we would take a swim, my mother would always know and I wondered how she got to know because I tried so hard to hide any evidence. One day I asked my mum how she knew and she disclosed to me that my eyes were always red after a swim and that my face and arms were dry and cracked. I would always receive a beating after a swim and after my mom disclosed to me how she got to know I stopped the whole business of swimming to the river. I learned that you cannot hide the truth and there will always be evidence left to show a wrong that you have committed. I now agree with those who say, that 'an old man can see far while seated on a chair than what a young boy can see while on top of a tree.'

My Lan T. Tran

SLEEP IS NOT OPTIONAL

ID: 331

I am a bit of a stress case; I will be the first to admit it. I tend to stay up long nights studying when I have an exam. However, I am beginning to think that this is not improving my performance on exams. Last semester I got about 2 hours of sleep for 3 nights in a row. I showed up for class with my shirt inside out and was such a mess that I spilled coffee all over my exam. I am starting to recognize that in order to properly function I need a certain amount of sleep. Next time, I will allow myself the luxury of a good night's sleep and I will almost guarantee that I will perform better on the next exam.

MAKE SURE THAT ALARM WILL WORK

ID: 129

I applied for a job once and was set to have an interview the next day. I was told to come at least 15 minutes early before the interview time so not to delay the process. I was so excited about this opportunity and reviewed some notes concerning the interview basics. I set my alarm clock two hours advanced of the specified time to allow myself to prepare well. And so I thought it would be. However, the next day, when I woke up it was only 30 minutes left before the interview time. My alarm clock had stopped at 3.00 am in the morning and did not work. The result, I was late for almost an hour for my most desired job interview. Luckily, I was still given the chance to have the interview but had waited several hours for an available slot. Though I was accepted as one of their trainee candidates, I still felt that I have given the company the impression of my poor time management, because the receptionist told me that no more tardiness should be expected from me in the duration of the training or I will automatically be removed from the project.

From that day on, I bought 2 alarm clocks to make sure that if one wouldn't work, the other likely would. I also have my cell phone's alarm to back

Mistakes In Life: The Path To Wisdom

them up just in case. True enough, I haven't had any late record anymore until I was officially accepted for the job.

PREPAREDNESS IS KEY

ID: 506

My school has something like a tradition during our first year. All freshmen go on a farm field trip. I'm a person who loves nature so I was excited. It was an amazing experience. I learned about different organic foods, and they even taught us how to make our own pizza made up of completely organic materials. It was delicious and could rival any fast food pizza joint in town. After lunch, then came the talk about the water-life in the farm and other things on that topic which I could not recall. After the talk, we all took a little hike and adventure. I didn't mind the hike. I loved the exercise and the smell of the ground still fresh from the rain. But, the part I dreaded was crossing a pond with no bridge in sight, just one log. One log connecting one side to the other. One log to walk on by putting one foot in front of the other. Here's another moment where I should have spoken up. Honestly, what was I thinking! I have horrible balance and I'm flat footed. That is not a good combination. My pride got in the way though, so I instead remained quiet and joined the rest of my class by crossing the log. I was almost on the other side when I suddenly lost balance and my leg ended up in the pond. It's good it wasn't deep, but the tour guide was talking about an alligator in the pond a few minutes before so I hurriedly crossed the remaining inches onto flat solid ground. Turns out there was a bridge a few minutes walk away. Turns out I forgot to pack an extra set of pants, so I walked around with one leg wet and the other one dry. I learned my lesson, you should always be prepared for all possibilities.

My Lan T. Tran

FETCHING FIREWOOD

ID: 63

Fetching firewood for cooking was a common chore for children when I was growing up because using gas for cooking was not known in rural areas. Whenever we would go to fetch the firewood, we would go for a swim too. Our parents were against swimming in the river though because some people had previously been attacked by snakes in that river. Oblivious of the danger, we couldn't miss out on the fun. One time my uncle followed us to the river, but we weren't aware of it. We undressed as usual and jumped into the river for a swim. My uncle took all our clothes and went home. After the swim, we went to get dressed only to find the clothes missing. We walked home naked and I found my mum waiting. I was punished for swimming despite several warnings I had been given. When your parents warn you of something, take heed and do as they say.

THE ORGMATE

ID: 361

One of the worst fallacies of youth is that we're often told that we are free to experiment with whatever we want. So in college, I did just that.

I was invited to join a department-based organization that handled my freshmen block. I was hesitant at first because applicants had to put in a lot of time and effort to get into these kinds of groups. The fact that I was swayed against my initial decision was based on two things: the organization promised academic support and their vice president kept on asking me to apply. To be honest, it was more of the latter reason than the former. She was cute and bubbly. When I failed to do certain tasks, when I was harassed by other members (all part of the application of course), she was there backing me up and making things easy for me. After one of the org's drinking parties, she asked me to spend the night at her apartment. I agreed partly because the dorm where I stayed closed its gate by midnight. Of course I also knew what her invitation meant. It was my first one-night-stand and I was thrilled that I didn't even have to put in a lot of effort for it. I was so proud that the next day, I even told one of my friends about it.

Mistakes In Life: The Path To Wisdom

After all, I went to a university that prided itself for having open-minded (and often eccentric) people. I thought it all ended with that one night.

But then she started texting me more often, asking personal questions and opening herself up as well. I felt uneasy. I thought it was clear for both of us. I tried distancing myself until one day, she just cried and told me she had feelings for me. FEELINGS! I should've known better. It's not that I'm a big jerk but at that time, I just wasn't open to commitments or relationships. I carefully explained my side and after sometime, we eventually became friends again. She may not have been clear about what she wanted, but then again, I shouldn't have capitalized on her vulnerability. I've never tried to have any similar experience since.

LEAKING FAUCET AND A HIGH WATER BILL...

ID: 167

I've been ignoring our dripping faucet for several weeks now and I haven't realized its effect until I received our monthly water bill. People at home were complaining of the annoying dripping noise which can be disturbing while you try to sleep. The actual reason why I kept on disregarding the idea of fixing it was firstly because I was too busy to do it. Another is that I didn't know how to fix it and if I hired someone to do the fixing, I surely would need to pay. At that moment we didn't have extra money for the job. So it was easier to hear regular complaints of the annoying dripping sound and ignore them, than to spend an extra dime to get rid of the problem. Until that is, I received a relatively high water bill at the end of that month and I realized that it was far better to fix it from the start than to pay at least 20% more than our regular monthly bill. After that bill, and after asking some friends and researching online of how to do it myself, I found out that it was easy to fix a dripping faucet! All I did was buy a new gasket for it, opened the nut which is the one located on the head of the faucet and changed the gasket. It took me less than an hour to fix it. Now there's no irritating dripping sound and no more high water bills.

My Lan T. Tran

DEPENDS ON YOURSELF NOT OTHERS
ID: 546

I was lazy, unwilling to do any work and I was proud about these bad habits. I used to copy my homework from my classmates. Naturally I have a charm that lets me control people by talking to them. I always used that to get my work done from others. Because of this, I started to depend on others. I could not do anything without anyone's help. My natural charm was not working well like before. As a result I soon fell into great danger. I could not complete any of my work. I understood what I had done to myself. By depending on others, I have become a useless person. I have learned that we need to try to do our work ourselves and we need to try our best. Otherwise there is no difference between us and chairs.

THE ONE DAY MILLIONAIRE HABIT
ID: 83

Nowadays, it is not only cash that gives us strong purchasing power; we now have credit cards. The credit limit alone will make you feel "rich" as this (based on Wikipedia – http://en.wikipedia.org/wiki/Credit_limit) is the maximum amount of credit that you are allowed to spend using your credit card.

Ever since 10 years ago, I had always been careful and meticulous in using my credit cards – I didn't spend them on things that I didn't need; I paid the total amount due in full; I tried my best to always keep it "credit-free." In other words, I used it ONLY when necessary – like when traveling internationally, or when buying stuff online. I had a very good credit standing with these banks, and they would occasionally offer me discounts and sale promos even if I didn't need or ask them.

For the past two or three years though, credit card companies have been very aggressive in encouraging their clients to spend, spend more, and spend to the max. The banks offered me 0% interest for 12-, 24-, and 36-monthly installments for single purchases for even as low as $100! They even have deals where you can convert your unused credit limit into cash,

Mistakes In Life: The Path To Wisdom

then pay the same in 12-, 24-, or 36- monthly installments with a minimal monthly interest of around 0.88% to 1.20%. Crazy huh?! I fell prey to this strategy, and it put me in really deep financial shit. Stupid me. I am now suffering the consequences. I lost track of my spending. Where I thought that a $500 item would be payable in 36 months – it turns out I am to pay $500 per month because I purchased several items worth several hundred dollars each! Insane. Stupid. Irresponsible.

When my debts started piling up and I could no longer even set aside a certain amount for my savings, I started getting worried. This gave me a really strong knock on the head. It's cool to be a millionaire – but only if you have it (literally). For now, I am slowly trying to catch up on all my debts. No need to explain it in detail but the major changes I've made to my "money spending habits" include:

- avoiding the malls as much as I can, but if I do go there, I strictly stick to my grocery/shopping list
- not taking my credit cards with me when I go out
- thinking twice, thrice, and even more, about each and every purchase I make (need versus want)
- throwing credit card offer letters away as soon as I receive them
- avoiding places that attract me to shop.

I still have a long way to go but I know I am getting there. I encourage you to do the same: Do not be a one-day millionaire (if you are not). Spend your money wisely.

NO HERO

ID: 337

I've always found it difficult to say "no" to a request, over time this really took a toll on me. This one particular week was really proving to be the busiest of the month. It was exam week, which meant as a teacher I had a small mountain of paper to check. My department head was on leave and had asked me to take over any meetings that might be scheduled while he was away and true enough there were. That week my mother also asked me to pick up my uncle who was arriving in our city. Now this was already beginning to look like a recipe for disaster.

The day before I was to pick up my uncle, our secretary informed me that I needed to meet with the Dean. I thought that I had it all under control; I just needed to maximize my time. The night before, I took to the task of checking my students' paper and went to bed late. When I woke up, it was already a quarter to 8 and I had to be at the Dean's office by 8. In a panic I rushed to get ready. But my uncle's flight arrived earlier than was scheduled and he was waiting for me for over 3 hours at the airport. I had also arrived too late to the meeting that the Dean had already lost her patience waiting for me.

That day I learned the value of asking for help. I am not some super woman who can do everything by myself. If only I had told my mom that I was too swamped with my work then she could've asked someone else to fetch him.

SALE? CHECK THE LABEL!

ID: 216

You know how the word SALE tickles you, specifically your "sense of shopping?" That happens to me a lot of times, especially in the grocery store. I sometimes feel that I am a hoarder, because I always make sure that there are always at least two extra stocks of whatever commodity I have in the house. Because of this, I also easily get attracted to the "SALE" sign because this means I save a lot when I buy several pieces of whatever.

So one day while shopping, I saw that huge SALE sign at the stand of the COKE ZERO's – my all time favorite soda. I usually buy 10 of these per month, so I went and checked it out. It was 40% off! I immediately dragged my husband to that isle and asked him to get 20 of those – hmm... wow... stock for two months! I never even got into that this-is-too-good-to-be-true dilemma.

Mistakes In Life: The Path To Wisdom

I almost forgot to buy the other stuff on my list, as the cart was already full and I guess I got too excited. Anyway, when it was time to line up at the cashier, I heard someone say that the sale items are "too good to be true." I thought… "What the heck, 40% off on my favorite soda? That's a very very good deal!"

Well it was my turn now. As I was transferring the goods to the cashier's deck, something caught my eye… the letters E X P. I quickly asked my husband what date it was, and found out that the expiration date was the next day! What a disappointment and disbelief! I almost wanted to go to someone and complain but realized… no one had done anything illegal YET. The goods were really not yet expired. No wonder it was on sale! So I immediately backed out of the line, and darted towards the COKE-ZERO-SALE lane. I put everything back into the display stand.

Though they say you can still consume the goods at almost a month after the expiration date, I still don't want to risk anything especially with food. Because of this experience, I am now more "paranoid" with sale items. I always make sure to look at the labels, specifically the Expiration Date.

AN ODE TO MY MOTHER

ID: 564

Last weekend, my mom and I went shopping together. Of course, we weren't the only ones there for it was Mother's Day. A huge crowd of people continued to gather on the department store where we walked for hours just to check every store we thought looked interesting to the both of us. My aunts, my grandma, my sister, my cousins and my husband came with us. We all had fun. After choosing some things to buy, we decided to eat together. Lately, I feel like it happens every month. I feel so blessed, happy and content that my life is so much better now. You might think that my life has always been this way however that is where you would be wrong. I, my friend, have experienced some tough times in the past. One of the biggest regrets in my life would have to be the time when I realized that my mother and I are not as close as we used to be.

My Lan T. Tran

"On April 1, 1985, a healthy baby girl was born. She was born to a young couple who both traveled to Libya to work there. Knowing that the Gulf War was starting and they needed to be safe from harm, the family flew back to their homeland in the Philippines to try and work there for several years once again. When the baby reached the age of 1, her mother knew it was time to move to another country. Unfortunately, due to the circumstances, she had to be left behind. At the age of 6, her father followed her mother to Oman. She cried as she did not understand why they were leaving her behind. She thought that they did not love her anymore. She was left in the guidance and care of her loving grandparents. That little girl grew up. At the age of 10, her parents went back to her to bring her to where they were. When she got there, she realized that she did not know her parents at all. It was like living with strangers except they aren't really."

By the way, the little girl that I mentioned earlier in the narration was me. I was just trying to give you an idea of how my life changed and how it was before. My mom tried hard to be close to me as she once was. I loved them growing up and I still love them deeply now but something was off, something was not right. Whether it was just a feeling that I should ignore or it was just something that I would grow out of, I knew I had to do something. I was their daughter after all. I tried my best to get close to her too but her constant working was something that I just had to understand. My parents were workaholics, you see, but I did not blame them for that. I know that they had good intentions and that they only did what they could to help us survive. My parents did not lavish me with attention or with gifts. Instead, they always tried to make time for me and my younger sister whenever they could. I had to learn to be independent at the age of 11. It was a harsh time but I was a grown up and knew that I should try to act like one.

I know my Mom was supposed to give me that talk about the birds and bees but somehow, it just never happened. Whether it was due to her busy schedule or due to something else, I do not know why. At the age of 17, I graduated from high school. Unfortunately, it was time for me to head back to where I came from as it was not easy to get the courses that I wanted to study in college from where I was. My parents hesitantly made me fly back home while they all stayed in a foreign country to earn what they could for me and for themselves. I was alone all over again. I missed them a lot.

Mistakes In Life: The Path To Wisdom

Despite the lateness of being with them, I was able to become close to them.

Perhaps blood is truly thicker than water. Now, that I was so far away, I just couldn't help but cry. I had to be tougher and stronger as I was going to be independent yet again. Without the guidance of an adult at that age was crucial. I made so many mistakes I feel like I cannot remember them all. That was one of the most troublesome parts of my life and I regret everything that happened then. Somehow I felt like I just needed my mother to give me a hug, pat my back and tell me that everything was going to be alright.

After everything that happened, my Mom went home to see me. She tried to understand me but I was a teenager with a lot of anger management issues and raging hormones. I was stubborn, reckless and impatient. I lacked the knowledge that I have with me now. My Mom and I often clashed. We argued about almost everything. I know she meant well but I always misunderstood her. Knowing what I did then makes me feel horrible. I feel like a bad daughter and that is what eats me. I know that I have hurt her so many times and have made her cry. I know whatever I have done in the past to pain her must be erased but memories stay forever, no matter how hard you try to make better new ones. I regret that I wasn't as loving as other daughters toward their mothers. Up until this day, it pained me to know that. My mother confessed to me about this before I got married in 2010. I was 25 then and she was not comfortable letting me go. She wanted me to stay with her longer but I felt like I was ready to move on with my life. I needed to add a new chapter to which she later understood.

I am 27 now and married. Although I do not have any kids yet, I intend to have one or two soon but before that happens I need to always make time for my mother. Even if she doesn't say it, I know she needs me. Although I live far away from her now, we call each other frequently, chat online or send messages to each other no matter how busy we both become. Perhaps because I am getting older and my Mom is too, I feel like our ages are starting to grow close to each other which somehow puts us in harmony now. Although I am still not at ease because I feel like I did lack in the past and am continuously lacking, at least, I am trying to make up for everything now. It is never too late to do something good to others and why will I start doing good to others when I should start doing it first to

My Lan T. Tran

those closest to me? This is a mother's day tribute to all the mothers out there. To my Mom, I am sorry for everything. I know I have said this a million times before but I love you and I hope that despite the distance that we have now and of course, the still evident differences, we will be able to put them all aside and conquer them all. Thank you for everything. You are the best. I love you!

DON'T USE VERY STRONG SHAMPOO
ID: 249

I have very limp hair. In my attempt to achieve the kind of hair that is full of volume and shine, I bought a shampoo which was endorsed by a renowned celebrity on a TV advertisement. Off I went and tried it for a week. I noticed that after I had been using it, an unusual thing happened – I had lots of hair falling out. I ignored it for a while because I must say, at some point my hair did get fuller than my normal hair. Weeks went on and then I began to develop an irritated and itchy scalp. My mother checked for me and told me she found blisters and hives all over. We both investigated the shampoo and discovered that it contained a number of tough chemical substances including formaldehyde. I learned that this can cause cancer. Since then I have switched to a regimen that doesn't rob the hair of its natural oils. Now I wash my hair with just a little amount of very mild or organic shampoo. I realized that I could still keep my hair healthy in sensible ways without using those compounds and cancer-causing agent.

LIVING A NEGATIVE FREE LIFE
ID: 441

I think I lived with a lot of negative people for the longest time. My friends from college found it easier to just put down my ideas when I discussed things with them. I started to see myself through their eyes – weak, soft, and quite unable to make good decisions, when as a matter of fact, deep inside I was burning with ambition and independence. I was conditioned by

Mistakes In Life: The Path To Wisdom

how my friends saw me, for example, when going grocery shopping, I always had difficulty choosing between two brands of a product. My reason for such is that I wanted to have good quality, but budget-friendly one. In their lack of patience in my behavior, one of them stomped his foot, "talked me down", said 'if you're not going to choose one now, we're going to leave you behind' and it was said in a condescending manner. I could manage to get home by myself but my love for my friends ruled over my pride. So I just closed my eyes and took the one I was holding in my right hand, depriving myself of the chance to choose I feared my friend who tell me off.

Over the years, I have met different people from all walks of life, traveled to a number of countries, and was friends with people that were more patient with me and more willing to give encouragement. It felt better inside that way and my relationships with them were not too stressful. I have been carrying all these years a crushed self-esteem from my younger days because of negative people around me. And I realized that it is just sad that most of them were friends I thought contributed to my wellbeing. But mind you, nothing was lost in the process because despite the negative friends I had before, I think I also learned a great deal about myself through them. I thought maybe the change should start within myself and that I should be able to express what I really feel inside rather than cowering down to another person's harsh behavior.

SAVE SOMETHING FOR YOUR FUTURE GENERATION

ID: 587

I have never thought that I would say something like this. Ever since my childhood I wasted so many things. I was careless about water, electricity or any kind of fuel or energy. Back then I thought like a fool, that the world had a vast resource of fuel.

But I was definitely wrong, and I realized that after attending an environment and energy related workshop. There I came to know about our environment and resources, there I learned, we don't have unlimited resources for energy. But everyday we are wasting energy and fuel in various ways.

But have we ever thought, what will happen if one day the resources are gone, what will the future generation do? You may say, they will find a way. But think to yourself, is that a perfect answer or you are leaving nothing for them!

Think more about it, here we are wasting and in the future they will suffer for our deed. Who thinks it's fair?

WISHING I HAD A PHONE

ID: 24

Many years ago when I was in elementary school, every time I walked around people they would always be talking about the new cell phones they had just gotten. Everyone I knew had a cell phone. I wanted to be like them so much that I had the guts to take my mom's cell phone and pretend it was mine. My mom woke up in the morning going around the house looking for it, asking me or my brother if we knew where it was. We had both said no. That day during school, I told everybody that I had gotten a new phone, showing it to them. To tell the truth it felt good being the center of attention. Upon coming home, I realized that I had forgotten to bring the phone home. Later, I had gotten my brother so mad, he ended up telling my mom and dad. After he had told them, I was in serious trouble, and now every time I ask for a cell phone they always tell me that once I get into college, they will buy me one. The lesson here is that if someone has something that you don't have, just forget about it. You might eventually get what you want, if you just ask.

Mistakes In Life: The Path To Wisdom

I GOTTA GO

ID: 106

Having kids teaches a parent more life lessons than could fill a book. One of the most memorable lessons that I have learned is that when a child says "Mom I gotta go," the car should be stopped immediately at a restaurant or gas station or in the woods. Kids cannot hold it, when they must pee, they must pee. This lesson was learned about two months after getting my new car. I had never had a new car and I took painstakingly good care of my four wheeled baby. On a trip home from the store my daughter was sitting in her booster seat and suddenly said, "Mom, I gotta go bad." I smiled and looked at her playing in the rearview mirror and said, "O.K. sweetie we will be home in just a few minutes." Little did I know that a few minutes was much too long. I focused on the road once again and within thirty seconds I heard the all too familiar sound of my daughter sniffing as she was trying to hold back tears. I glanced back to see an ever spreading puddle in her booster seats and on my new car seat. My heart fell as I realized that my back seat had officially been christened. My new four wheeled baby was now a family car, complete with urine stain. I did not get angry at my daughter, after all she told me she had to go badly. I also learned that children are usually brutally honest and if they say they need to go, then a sudden stop should be made.

ENJOY LIFE, HAVE A BREAK

ID: 478

I have always been grade conscious. I always wanted to be somewhere near the top of the class, it made me feel capable. From high school to college, I strived to maintain this status quo. I stressed myself out a lot whenever I failed, and I studied like crazy to pull up my grades. At the end of the day, I always had good grades. But, I should have tried being more social. I missed out on many parties. I missed out on a lot of inside jokes. I missed out on a lot of fun moments. I realized this 2 years before I finished college. So, I took that one step and finally said yes. Yes, I'll go. It was really fun, and it was a good way to relieve some stress. I needed to laugh. I needed to walk around. I needed to have those random talks wherein anything and everything came up. It was fun, and I'm glad it wasn't too late before I realized it. Grades are important, but so are you. You have to treat yourself and relax once in a while. Enjoy life, don't waste it by staring into the deep abyss of information your books provide you every single day. Take a break and manage your time, that's all you need to be a happy student not just a studious one.

TRAVELING WITH MOM

ID: 306

I'm 29 years old and my mother is 73 years old. I recently took her on vacation with me. There were portions of this trip where we had to do quite a bit of walking. There were times when I forgot how old my mother was and kept on pressing her to continue walking and got cranky at her for being so weak. Then on our way back one night we had to take a ferry and the boat was rocking side to side all the way. Before I knew it I was having a terrible case of seasickness, however my mother didn't, not even one bit. My mother never once complained or got cranky at me for being such a wuss for getting seasick. She played rock, paper, and scissors with me and sang with me, etc... through the entire ferry ride to help alleviate my motion sickness. I felt really bad after that. I'm trying harder to be patient with her and be more aware of her health and assist her rather than keep pushing her because she's not that young anymore.

WEDDING

ID: 48

Whenever I would attend a wedding with my friends, we expected to eat to our fill and also have a share of the cake. There was one time that I attended a wedding but I delayed in queuing myself to be served food and it happened that I was among the last guests in the queue. As I approached the serving place it was clear that the food was very minimal and chances of missing it were very high. Sure enough, when I got there, food was over and the chef just told me "sorry, you're unlucky today". I felt embarrassed because I had already washed my hands to eat the food. I went home hungry, having to trek 5km on an empty stomach. From that day on, I promised myself that I would always be the first when it comes to queuing for food at a social gathering, if I intend to have some food. It's better to be first than last in whatever you want to achieve. Be a go getter in whatever you desire to obtain.

SOME RULES ARE NOT MEANT TO BE BROKEN

ID: 333

My parents were very strict, so unlike a lot of other kids in my high school I did not get my license until I was 18 years old. Since I hadn't had much freedom before, as soon as I took a car out alone for the first time, I decided it was my chance to cut loose. I drove at ridiculously fast speeds, 10, 20 sometimes even 30 miles over the speed limit. I got away with it for a while, but it caught up with me. I got my first ticket for doing 15 miles over the speed limit, and my second only a few months later for 20 miles over. By the time I was finished driving like a crazy person all of the time, I had received around 5 tickets, and lost my license for 3 months. I learned very quickly (while my dad drove me around everywhere just like I used to have him do) that there are some rules out there that are very important to follow.

DON'T EAT THE COOKIES

ID: 131

My aunt is a true prankster and a horrible cook and though the two were at one time mutually exclusive, a few years ago they came together. My aunt, in a prank war with several of us at a time, brought in some cute little cookies that were well iced and looked very tasty. She set them on the table at the office and said nothing other than I brought cookies. It was not unusual for someone to bring in left over snacks from home so this was not out of the ordinary. All day we went back and forth and everyone tried a cookie, but no one said much. I grabbed my own right before lunch and popped the small square into my mouth. I immediately spit it back out. My aunt had always been a bad cook, but this was a new low, the cookies were rock hard and the icing did little to hide the taste. I waited all day before I finally had the nerve to ask her exactly what those cookies were supposed to have been. She grinned and started laughing. She said , "Oh they were meant to be a hilarious prank." I knew she had won the war as she explained that the 'cookies' had been dog treats that were covered in icing. My lesson learned was to always know your enemy when in a prank war and to always make sure your cookies are not made by Alpo.

DEFINITELY NEVER GOING TO ACT
ID: 507

Sometimes, people think of me too highly. I will never really understand why they see me as such a capable and responsible person. It scares me a lot to have a lot of hopes and expectations on my shoulders. In my first year of high school, I was chosen to play the lead in a school play. I've never acted, I'm quite shy, and I thought there was someone much more capable. But still, they chose me. I tried my best to try to not let them down but it didn't matter. It was on the fated day of the presentation of the play that I realized, I have stage fright. The play was a long one and my character had such long monologues. To add to that, my group was the first to perform. Nerve-wrecking, blinding, heart-racing, and finally mind blanking. I blanked out around halfway through the play. I could not remember my lines. The stage was small, and it would be obvious if someone tried to feed me my lines so I tried to wing it. No one said it outright after the play, but that was a disaster. I apologized to my group for choking under the pressure, and being the great people they were they said it was okay. We were still able to finish everything which is what mattered. I think I should have spoken up and not let them cast me for that part. I'm glad though that despite my shortcomings, I was at least able to deliver most lines and tried to stay in character despite the panic. I never want to experience that again though, next time I'll just refuse and opt for a job behind the scenes.

YOU FEAR THAT (TINY) THING? o.O

ID: 64

My young niece, like many other kids who were born in America, has a fear for spiders. I don't. Often times she would make a big deal at the sight of the tiniest spiders and run away. One day I got really upset and I yelled at her and told her to cut it out. In my angry voice I said "LOOK at the size of that spider and LOOK at yourself! You're a MILLION times larger than it. It's harmless!! You're freaking over something that's like nothing!!!" She had tears in her eyes trying to control her fear and not running away from it.

Then one day I was working in the backyard, picking up tiles left laying on the grounds for months. When I got towards the bottom of the pile I picked one up and saw this orange-yellowish centipede look-a-like I SCREAMED my head off for a couple minutes and I think my entire neighborhood heard me. I almost passed out from the sight of it as if I had seen a ghost. That thing was probably 10 times smaller than the tiniest spider my niece often saw. I have a distinct hate/fear for creatures with many legs! After I calmed down, I remembered my niece and when I yelled at her about the spider. I felt really bad so we had a talk and I apologized. The lesson here is try to be sympathetic towards people and try to understand that not everyone has the same fear towards certain things as you do.

2ND CHANCES

ID: 365

Since I was a kid, I was never close with my dad. He and my mom got their marriage annulled when I was young due to unsettled differences. As a result, I spent my weekdays with my mom and got to go to his place during weekends and some holidays. We then got separated for five years after he decided to work in Japan to raise capital.

When he got back in 1999, our relationship was strained. We weren't used to being around each other anymore. I had no clear memory of what he was like. He was absent during my formative years. We would fight over petty things like me being late when I would come to visit him, or if I didn't answer his calls immediately. For a while, I hated him because of the way he spoke to me. This strain went on undiscussed and eventually the resentments just snowballed through the years.

Then in 2009, after I got home from a trip to the US, he was admitted to a hospital. I complained about having to stay and take care of him since as a kid, I remembered he never wanted to spend the night at a hospital with me when I was the one sick. I had no choice but to be there though because I was his closest family member. I had no siblings and he never remarried. A few days later, while I was away on some errand, he was rushed to the ICU after falling into a coma-like state. The doctors said certain minerals drastically dropped from his system after taking a crash-diet course that eventually led to the condition that affected his brain. No one expected a recovery. It was the only time I cried while I was near him.

I cried because there were so many things I wanted to tell him. I wanted to say how proud I was of him for toughing it out abroad away from his family just to provide for our needs. I wanted to tell him that while he may have always been a case of tough-love, I understood the things he didn't say when we had arguments and he picked hurtful words instead.

Luckily, we were given a second chance. The recovery was slow; his speech was impaired for a while. Even his memory was effected as he could not distinguish reality from things he imagined every now and then. But I never took that second chance for granted. I was patient with him when he had bad days, and I opened up to him when he had good ones.

As people often say, we should live each day like it's our last. Not all of us are guaranteed second chances. Let's not wait for instances like this before we show people how much they're appreciated.

Mistakes In Life: The Path To Wisdom

GET OUT OF THE MUD

ID: 171

My first year teaching full time was spent in kindergarten. I wanted to look overly professional as a first year teacher so I wore my best skirts and heels to work every morning. This isn't saying much since I was a new teacher and even as a seasoned teacher we make very little money. So there I was facing a room full of five year olds in heels and a dress. Within the first week I learned why kindergarten teachers are rarely in skirts and never in heels. Aside from the fact that these little children are much shorter than you already and chairs are tiny, heels make you unsteady around fast moving little bodies. Skirts are hard to wear when most of your time is spent in miniature furniture and on the floor, but the real lesson was learned that first week on the playground. Every day before it was time to load the buses the kindergarten classes traipsed to the playground for some free time. My time was mostly spent on the end of the playground watching the small soccer area and saying stay out of the mud. The end of the first week could not come fast enough. I was exhausted, little did I know I would go out with a bang or should I say a splash. Minutes before we were headed in on the Friday afternoon I heard that noise every teacher dreads, that of a child crying. A crying child on a playground usually means someone is hurt and sure enough one of the little ones was on the ground holding her leg. I headed over to the spot and my heel suddenly decided to stop without me, sending me face first into the mud that I had asked the kids to repeatedly stay out of each day. I laid there for a moment and then started laughing. My only other choice was to cry. The other teachers ran over and to my surprise the crying child had been silenced and over taken by the urge to laugh at her now mud covered teacher. I got up pulled my mud covered shoes off and entered our school barefoot, more than embarrassed. I never wore another pair of heels after that day. In fact I am not even sure that I own a pair now. That week was when I learned that kindergarten, mud, and heels do not mix.

My Lan T. Tran

DON'T SMOKE

ID: 547

I was 15 when I first tried smoking. I was on a picnic. Some of my friends and me made out and smoked. We found it to be a game. That was the first time I tried smoking. I felt it quite fascinating and stylish. So soon I started to do it again and again. Over time I felt addicted to smoking. I couldn't help but smoke at least twice a day. Soon the numbers increased. Time by time it became bigger. I eventually had to smoke 15 to 20 cigarettes a day. I could not stop myself from smoking. As a result I found that my lungs were not okay anymore. I sat with a doctor, & after checking me he said I am still quite good but I will not be if I continue smoking at this rate. He suggested I give up smoking. But it was not that easy. I was also inspired with one of his speeches "Smoking doesn't only harm the smoker but also people around him". Hearing that, I promised I would give up smoking. And I am trying my best to keep that promise. Now I don't smoke as often, and I am sure the day is very close when I will give it up completely.

CURIOSITY DID NOT KILL THE CAT...IT SCARED ME OFF

ID: 89

When I was a kid, I loved to watch my parents do their daily preparations for work: my mom preparing her office clothes, blow drying her hair, and putting her contact lenses on; my dad shaving his beard, putting on his favorite cologne, and sorting the documents that he has to take to the office. Out of all these things I got to witness on Saturdays (because this is the only day I can stay in bed and watch them), my amusement was focused on my dad's shaver. I was really curious on how all the facial hair almost disappears after that tiny gadget glides on his face. My story is about this small "amusing and magical gadget."

I was six years old, my younger brother was four. We loved tinkering with stuff in our parents' drawers and trying stuff as we had seen them use it. One Saturday while my brother was playing his Game & Watch (for those of

Mistakes In Life: The Path To Wisdom

you who don't know >> http://en.wikipedia.org/wiki/Game_%26_Watch), my eyes got fixated on THAT silver magical gadget of my dad's. I had doubts taking it from the drawer because dad once told me that it was not for kids. Being the stubborn kid that I was though, I picked it up, and started thinking about where to "glide" the thing. Hmmm... I didn't try it on myself because I wouldn't see it... so... without even thinking, I used it on my brother's hair, right at the top of his head! I was so having fun that the shaved part became as big as a match box. I stopped when I saw lots of hair falling on the floor. My poor innocent brother didn't know what was going on, he didn't even notice it was his hair on the floor. At this point when I saw the bald patch on his head, I started worrying, and even tried to pick the hair up and put it back. It didn't stay though! I didn't find the patch funny at all, I started to cry because I thought I hurt him. Our nanny rushed towards the room and instantly, she saw the bald patch. I remember she pinched my arm and grabbed my brother towards her. She also took the shaver from me and started scolding me. I don't remember what happened after this, but I surely won't forget that this is one of the very few times that my dad scolded me. He said I might have hurt my brother if I hadn't stopped.

I realized that the patch really looked awful and so the next day, which was a Sunday, we took my brother to the barbers and he had to get that "military" style haircut where almost no hair remains. I felt bad, really bad, even the barber talked to me about it.

Looking back at what happened, (the patch I now find really funny because I vividly remember what it looked like) I realized that small things like this really do impact your life and they eventually get connected to some adult-life experiences. What I learned from this is to ALWAYS THINK BEFORE YOU ACT and to NOT DO TO OTHERS WHAT YOU DON'T WANT DONE TO YOU. On the practical side, I'd say that parents should always keep unsafe gadgets away from children's reach, and that for parents too – every time your kid asks you a question, try your best to answer in the most basic and detailed way ... not just saying "No you can't do that because that is bad."

My Lan T. Tran

DON'T BE A THIEF

ID: 396

I was 16 then when my mother left me so that she could work in another country. I was so scared at that time because I felt so alone. In order for me to overcome my fear, I joined a social sorority in our school. All of my allowances were spent in all that nonsense. My allowance for a week was not enough to go out with my sorority friends. My mother increased my allowance because I told her that I had a project. I fooled my mother and I didn't save anything. I just wasted everything she gave me and I forgot to care about the hardship that she had undergone in her job. I then realized that I needed to save some amount of money so that my mother would also be happy. Don't be a thief to the effort of your parents because it won't lead you to a better future.

DO WHAT YOUR DOCTOR SAYS

ID: 211

If you talk about thriftiness, I think it is my middle name. I always look for ways in order to save and always look for something that is a little less from the regular price. But I learned my lesson not to overdo it a while back when I was sick with a respiratory infection and had been prescribed with several antibiotics by my doctor. Some of the medicines were too expensive to be taken 3 times a day in 7 days. For the intention of saving, I decided to buy the generic instead of the branded medicines that my Doctor had insisted me. That way, I could complete all the meds in 7 days. However, because of poor quality, instead of getting rid of my sickness in 7 days, I still didn't feel well. So I went back to my Doctor, compulsory to say the truth of what I did and was reprimanded that I needed to take exactly the ones he prescribed to assure treatment of my ailment. So then I finally did what was advised and in a few days I was much better but ended up spending more than I would've if I had taken my physician's advice the first time. Saving when it comes to curing your illness is not a good idea after all. I make sure now to follow what's exactly being prescribed by my Doctor.

Mistakes In Life: The Path To Wisdom

I COULD HAVE AVOIDED THAT

ID: 565

It was the last night of 2011, the 31st night. My friends and I were preparing to celebrate the new year and say goodbye to 2011. As it was the time of winter, we planned to get drunk, fully drunk that night. So according to our plan, we bought two one liter bottles of absolute Vodka and one bottle of local whiskey for four of us. I don't drink regularly, actually I don't drink much. But at that time I was going crazy along with my friends. So I drank at the party with great pleasure. But after finishing two bottles of Vodka, I lost control and vomited on the bed. I was really ashamed of my deed. I knew, I couldn't take that much, but I didn't avoid that. And that brought me sufferings.

I'M BUSY, GO AWAY!

ID: 250

I have 3 nieces that grew up with me since birth. I moved away after I got a job and they would come stay with me during summer time and school breaks. We would play Monopoly, Poker, see movies, cook together, play games/sports, take trips here and there for fun, sleep together, etc... There weren't many good times because I was mostly busy working. Three days ago on Christmas, before I left my sister's house to go back home I was expecting all three of my nieces to come with me for a few days, but to my surprise the youngest teenage niece was staying back so she could do stuff with her friends. I was beyond furious because our time together was limited and now she was putting friends before family. My anger calmed down when I suddenly remembered all those times when she was at my house and would come knocking on the door asking me to come play with her and I would refuse and send her away. I told her I was busy working and closed the door on her. That made me feel really sad. She's grown up so quickly and time flew by so fast. Luckily, she was able to reschedule events with her friends and her mom saw how sad she was and drove her up to my house several hours later. That made me very happy. I'm going to spend more time with family from now on, especially the ones who aren't going to be alive much longer and the ones moving away to college soon.

My Lan T. Tran

IV INSERTION

ID: 443

It was my first time being assigned as an IV nurse; all I needed to do was to do an IV insertion to those who were newly admitted patients and to those who had any inflammation or edema in their IV site. I also followed up their IV fluids. There was really an unusual thing that happened during my shift. I made a mistake inserting an IV catheter to a wrong patient. I was really so sleepy during that time, which was why I wasn't able to see the exact name of the patient to whom I did the insertion. That patient whom I inserted an IV catheter into happened to have the same family name with the patient on the right. I realized that I should not be tardy when going on duty. I really needed to be alert so that what happened to me that night will never happen again. I hope to be fully conscious when doing night shift duty. I learned to take some vitamins and have enough sleep and rest.

BE FAITHFUL

ID: 588

It was two years ago since this event happened. When I was a second year university student, my mother sent 30 dollars for educational support. I went to the bank to receive the money. I got to the bank and completed all the processes required. Then I waited for a while till customers who had come before completed their task. When he called my name I gave him my ID and after he had checked it, he returned my ID and gave me the money. At that moment, I did not check the amount but put it in my pocket and directly left. After that I went to my dorm and when I counted the money, It was $50. I was amazed and thought that this was my chance that God gave me. I told my friends about the entire scene. Some of them advised me to return the extra money since it is a sin and not expected from me to have others property as one's own. The other friends psychologically forced me not to give the money back. Then my mind battled with two worlds, to give back or not to give. Then I decided to take the money for my own interest. After a long period of time, someone stole a lot of money from my pocket. I couldn't control myself …. I said 'to whom shall I tell this to? God can't hear me since I had done the same mistake before...' From

Mistakes In Life: The Path To Wisdom

this event I learned that I don't have to own money that is not mine and realized that I will be in trouble as I made trouble before.

POVERTY

ID: 26

During my childhood years in primary school, our family was struggling to make ends meet and therefore we couldn't afford most luxuries. Our neighbors were well off and could afford a good life. They could afford to have bread every morning for breakfast while we only had tea. There was a favorite meal that we only had an opportunity to eat during Christmas time, but to our neighbors it was a meal like any other. Whenever they were preparing the meal, I would make abrupt visits with my other siblings just to see if we could be offered the 'chapatti' but sometimes they would deny us a chance to even taste it. This made me hate poverty because it denied me the chance to have what the better families could easily afford. I swore to myself that I would work very hard in school to ensure I got good grades that would give me a chance to go to a university, and get myself a good job to ensure I would enjoy what I lacked as a child. I also swore I'd give the best to my kids and help my other siblings have a good life too. I made it and I learned that poverty is not permanent. We all have an opportunity to get rid of it eventually.

IF YOU ARE NOT FAMILIAR, GO WITH THE USUAL

ID: 107

I was invited once to an Indian restaurant to dine with the clients. The Operations Manager of the company I worked for had asked me and my manager to join our three clients with their lunch break. So my boss chose one of the Indian restaurants in our place considering that we have visitors from India. During the order taking, my boss had told me to order what I'd like to eat. So I browsed on the menu and had initially decided to go for the Indian dish that I was familiar with, however, I saw one dish that looked deliciously enticing on the picture. So, I went ahead and ordered the food. When our food was served, I noticed that what I ordered was somewhat different looking in reality. It had a considerable amount of red chili pepper. The food tasted fine however it was very spicy. I'm not really fond of spicy foods, so what happened was I forced myself to eat it and pretended to like it, just so not to get any attention from my boss and the clients. After that lunch meeting, I had drunk several glasses of water just to get rid of the spicy after taste.

Now, if I'm dining with the bosses in a new restaurant and trying to impress them, I go for the food that I'm familiar with or at least read the food description very well. I don't force myself to eat foods I don't like anymore.

A FEW STOLEN MOMENTS

ID: 479

The internet is the best tool for deception; wearing a mask is not necessary to stay incognito. The fact that nobody will know who the real person is behind the screen is enough for anybody to deceive someone, most especially women. More often than not, those who are in search of carnal pleasure are hunting women online through social dating. I have been a victim of this. I met this guy online. We became chat pals for more than a year. At first it was just a casual chat, which later developed into a passing fancy.

I never expected that out of the blue it would develop into something deep and intimate. After a year of spontaneous chatting, phone calls, and sending SMS every once in a while; we finally decided to meet personally; that first meeting led to several meetings until the inevitable thing happened. We did quench our physical longings and yearnings for each other, not just once or twice, but until the time he admitted was very much married with two young kids.

Mistakes In Life: The Path To Wisdom

I felt as if the whole world was crumbling down on me at that time. I felt so devastated and furious for my stupidity. I was so gullible that I never even doubted that those moments we had were just a few stolen moments. It took me more than a year to bounce back to life and heal the pain. It nearly ruined my entire life. But because of my very supportive friends, I feel vindicated and found the courage to move on. That's why I am here now telling my story with no more pain and without a heavy heart. I just regret that I had wasted those moments of my life with a Bastard.

Lesson: Do not be too trusting, most especially those people you meet online. It is better to date somebody from your neighborhood to avoid being deceived.

STRESS RUINED MY RELATIONSHIP

ID: 307

There was a period in my life when I always got so angry and frustrated that sometimes I ended up shouting and kicking objects. It was becoming a serious problem and it affected my relationship with my family and friends. I only noticed it when during that time in my life I also lost my boyfriend because of my temperamental attitude. I then decided to go seek some help and realized that intense stress at work caused it. I faced too much pressure and demanded more than I could handle and didn't know how to counteract the stress. I also suffered from lack of sleep for a while. I was recommended to take stress management lessons and learned some good stress relieving techniques like engaging into sports, exercise, going out more with friends and seeing new places during my free time. Eventually, I had noticed that the more I did these activities, the more relaxed I got and the less likely I was to blow a fuse. I can handle stress and pressure well now. I guess all we need is to recognize that we have a problem and do something to correct and solve it.

My Lan T. Tran

CAR ACCIDENT

ID: 50

When I was in college, I had a nice car bought for me by my family. [Technically, the brother who wrote the check didn't know that the other brother had convinced me to buy the car]. I can normally multitask while driving like eating, shifting gears and speeding, looking out for cops, and talking on the cell phone all at the same time. One particular day during wintertime, I drove my friend home after having studied together. On the way home I multitasked again and I was so busy talking to her that I wasn't aware that we had taken a turn from a big road onto a small road where the snow wasn't thoroughly plowed and some was still on the ground. When I got to the curve I was going a bit too fast and I couldn't stop in time and I slid and slammed hard into a parked car. I didn't get hurt, but my friend did, luckily not too much. My car insurance shot up to above $4000 (yes four thousand) per year. I got yelled at big time by the brother who paid for the car. Luckily, I had a sister who loved me very much and every month she would pay that heavy car insurance bill for me. The lesson here is talk a little less while driving and pay more attention to the road, especially during winter time, doesn't matter how good of a driver you think you are. Accidents are bound to happen if you're not careful. It is neither cool nor smart to multitask while driving. It's a miracle I'm still alive and in one piece. If you don't love yourself enough to take the advice, then love your family and friends and don't let them pay the price for you. And if you can, take your car to a big empty parking lot and practice driving on snow. Accelerate it, brake it, turn while accelerating, turn while braking, etc... let it slide, feel it slide so you have a better understanding of how your car handles on the snow. Don't do it so much that you flip the car over or crash though.

UNSAFE BABY BATH

ID: 255

I was so excited to be a mom for the first time that I bought every single baby product I could find. For my baby's first bath, I had for him a warm bath with fruity bubble bath. He seemed to enjoy his regular wash until I discovered my baby's skin had blotches on his arms and parts of his body. I checked with our pediatrician and she said it could have been allergic skin reaction caused by the materials or products used by my child. She said linens, beddings, and crib covers could sometimes have components which irritate the skin. I doubted it because I only bought hypoallergenic stuff for my baby. I went through every single one of his clothes, diapers, shampoo, baby bath, and even his baby powder. I discovered the culprit was the fruity baby bath. Although it claimed to be mild for baby's skin, the contents tell otherwise; it is composed of strong substances such as unacceptable amounts of Paraben and Methylparaben. These make the product have longer shelf life, but isn't safe at all when it gets into contact with a baby's skin especially. I ditched it altogether and opted for natural washing up foam that did not contain the things which were harmful for my baby. Also, I am wary more than ever now concerning his stuff; I read the label and ingredients very carefully before purchasing them.

DON'T OVERDRESS IT

ID: 133

I was invited to a party once by a schoolmate and I thought it was cool to go and meet new people. I was excited because I knew of several friends that would also join the bash. It was my friend's sister's dinner party. I knew the place so I decided to go directly to the place without asking my friend of any details. I thought I should wear a formal dress to be pleasant looking. As a plan, I have to go there a little late to make sure that everybody or at least a lot of people were already at the place before me. And so I did, when I got there wearing a gown, I was shocked that everybody was only wearing casual attires. Most of them were wearing shirt and jeans, not even close to my dress. I felt so embarrassed and off from the crowd. Everybody had their eyes on me and were obviously stunned and amused at the same time. As for me, I just stayed for few minutes and left. Until now, I haven't gotten over from that embarrassing experience. I totally made fun of myself. But now, every time I'm invited to any event or going to somewhere, I make sure I have all the details before going.

My Lan T. Tran

NURTURING A CHILD

ID: 508

It is true that love begets love. This I can prove with my son; the minute I gave birth to him, my heart was full of love that, all of my affection was poured down unto him. I promised that all of my mistakes in rearing his elder sister would never be done to him. However, as he grew up, there were always those times when I could not control my temper; thus I would snap at him from time to time.

Years passed until it was time for him to go to early childhood school. Compared to his sister, my son is quite slow. Like my father I always wanted the best performance from my kids. Since he was slow in writing every night I taught him to write. But perhaps it was too difficult for him to do it so I ended up shouting and hitting him which made him more nervous and confused. As a result he could not even write even one single straight line.

When he would fall asleep, I felt so sorry for what I had done and promised not to do it again; however, every time I taught him I could not control my temper. As months passed by, I noticed that his school performance was too low. So I searched on the net for things I must do to make him improve. There, I found lots of tips in parenting, disciplining and most of all making a child to become an Ace in the class.

I tried my best to be calm when teaching him his lessons, but the most effective technique was to let him discover his ability on his own. I just give him a worksheet to work on, and then check his mistakes. Surprisingly, it worked; now I am only reminding him to study but I don't interfere unless he asks for my help.

Lesson: As a mom, I must be there to support my kid's needs not to become a threat. Soothing, calm and comforting words are better than snapping and shouting at them. Constant yelling will just make them stubborn and hard-headed, whereas talking to them in a calm and diplomatic manner always makes sense.

Mistakes In Life: The Path To Wisdom

SINCE WHEN WAS FACEBOOK HOMEWORK?

ID: 65

I come from a family of very strict parents, so I lived by the rule. The basic rule was that when you get home from school, go take a shower, come down and do your homework. So I started doing my homework, until I got bored so I logged into my Facebook account and just started talking to people. From where I was sitting I could hear if anybody was coming, so I was able to close the window just in time for them not to see. HOWEVER, on this particular day, my dad must have tip-toed or something because I couldn't hear him walking. My brother was behind me and whispered to me "dad", so I quickly closed the window thinking he wouldn't see, but was I wrong. He stomped into the room, and asked me what I was doing. Stupidly I replied, "I'm doing my homework." Then he asked me since when was Facebook homework? So I ended up getting in a lot trouble, and he started to yell at me for what felt like hours but was a couple of minutes. Lesson learned if you have work to do, I suggest you finish it before doing anything, because it can always get you in trouble.

I'M GETTING TOO OLD FOR THIS

ID: 366

I used to drink a lot more in my teens and 20's. Now I am married and in my 30's and don't drink much at all. For one thing, I am usually the designated driver. Another reason is that I just get too silly. I am very lightweight and one or two drinks make me lippy. Case in point: I was out with my hockey teammates the other day and I was drinking after a long period without alcohol. It was only 2 drinks but I had an empty stomach. I don't even remember what I said but I know it was sexually explicit and it made my (male) teammates' jaws drop. So now I am no longer the quiet married girl on the hockey team – I am the foul-mouthed trucker that can't handle her alcohol.

My Lan T. Tran

HOT COFFEE VS. TONGUE

ID: 172

I visited a friend's house once and was offered a cup of coffee. I remember that I hadn't had any that day so the nice sweet aroma of it enticed me to take an immediate sip. You may have guessed that the coffee was maybe too hot but I was stupid to not expect this and had burnt my tongue after that sip. I was too embarrassed to admit to my friend about the incident so I let the coffee set warm before drinking it again. I finished drinking the coffee however when I went home, I saw that my tongue seemed to have turned very red and had a little white patch on it. It appeared to be a blister on my tongue. It hurt every time food touched my mouth and I couldn't properly taste anything. After a couple of days though, it healed itself. I really make sure to blow on my food or drink now before tasting them. And also always use your sense of touch first to know if it's hot or not.

DRIVE CAREFULLY

ID: 548

I like to ride bikes. I don't have any personal bike but my father has got two. I used to ride as fast as I could. Riding faster always made me feel a sense of fascination and a lot of pleasure. I used to play with the bike, when I rode on it. I used to race with my friends and I was very careless. Sometimes I lured unknown people to race with me. I didn't care about if I failed to control it and caused serious accidents.

One day I was going to the nearby town with my friend. Both of us were riding bikes and his younger sister was riding with him. I lured him to race with me, but he refused to race having his sister sitting on his bike. But I was not so thoughtful. I was rather determined to make him race me. Every time he denied, my determination increased more. But he was also determined not to race. Then I thought that even though he was rejecting me, he would try to catch me if I start to drive very fast. I started to drive faster than usual. He was not as fast, but also tried to keep a little distance from me. Because of that he had to drive faster than usual, but not that fast. As we were passing the curved roads, he asked me to drive slowly. I

Mistakes In Life: The Path To Wisdom

didn't listen to him. I wish I had listened to him. Another fast biker was coming from the opposite side of the road. Seeing him coming, I lessened my speed, but my friend couldn't see him coming as he was right behind me. As a result there was a terrible accident. Both my friend and the other biker got seriously injured, and my friend's sister was injured too. But it was not their fault, although I was not injured. That accident made me change. Now I think, there is no pride in fast riding, it's only the same. So ride carefully, don't become too ruthless.

DON'T DRINK AND SPEAK

ID: 88

I attended a childhood friend's party once and had enjoyed myself very much. I did drink a little too much and to my dismay I had said some words that were not meant to be said. One of my friend's guests, who I thought was weird-looking had been a victim of my rudeness. He had the biggest set of eyes I had ever seen and his nose didn't compliment them as it was too small and flat for his face. I am not usually a rude person when I have a clear mind and always careful of my words around people, however that night was a disaster. I was not able to hold what my thoughts really were when that guy joined our group chatter. I told him how weird-looking he was and everyone heard it. I was not even through with that. I went into the details of his features and worst, I told him that no one would ever be friends with a guy like him. I learned what I had done when my friend told me the next day. My friend also said that she was embarrassed of what I had done that night and that the guy was his cousin. I also learned that everything I had said was heard by her family and that they were furious with me.

After that, my friend avoided me and did not talk to me for several months. I was also not invited to her house or to any of her family's party ever since. Later we talked to each other but I haven't made up with her family yet. The worst part is the way it made me feel as a person. I regarded myself as the most arrogant and insensitive individual by doing that. And that incident will always put a bad record on my character. From that night onwards, I always remember not to drink too much as not to lose my "good self".

A MOTHER'S LOVE

ID: 399

Ever since I was a young child, my mom spoiled me. Toys, clothes, or food, I got everything. For my mom, a child's happiness is more important than her own,

I grew up and became a teenager, still getting spoiled by my mom. I was the youngest, and she seldom got mad at me. Every time I got good grades, I got treated to the mall or she would give me money. I got so used to it that I took it for granted.

As I grew older, I got fond of different vices. I got addicted to parties and alcohol. I always got home late, but she never scolded me. I failed my grades, but she always gave me second chances. Until one day, she finally got the courage to scold me. I totally lost myself and I fought back. She had a heart attack.

I almost fainted. I never meant to do it to my mom. What others say is definitely true, when someone is at the point of breaking, that's the only time you recognize how you truly care for them. I cried so hard that I wanted to scream. How could I have done all those things to her? From then on, I promised myself to change myself. Thanks to my mother's love, I am where I am now. Living happily and content.

SAVING MONEY GONE WRONG

ID: 213

We hit a financial hurdle a few months ago and to save money, I offered to dye my own hair rather than go to a salon. I take pride in my long, wavy, blond hair, which I usually put a few highlights in to go even blonder. I bought a $15 box of dye and was proud that I could save almost $140 on my hair. Then, after following all instructions, I washed the dye out and found myself with orange hair. I was mortified. For the first time in my life, I called into work "ugly" (not sick!). I ended up at the salon right when it opened and as luck would have it, my stylist could see me. She fixed up my mistake and I showed up at work 4 hours later and $165 poorer.

Ladies, unless you know what you are doing – don't try and dye your own hair!

TO SHARE OR NOT TO SHARE

ID: 566

It was all very subtle at the beginning when I started out with my new employer. It was a new industry and the approach to sales and marketing was not what I was used to. At the beginning I kept telling myself that it was a new challenge and I would learn a lot out of it. With this statement it was all too clear that I was thinking about soft skills that I could easily use elsewhere and most importantly, my resume will not have a gap.

I kept on learning and interacting with clients who had a very technical approach to work and the learning was hands on and I kept convincing myself that I was going to use the skills I gained in the field I wanted. I did use that platform to gain and experiment on things I read online or trends in the industry and some worked, others failed.

Then came the pressures of attaining certain goals which as my boss came to tell me I barely reached half of what he had expected of me. This should have been my cue to wake up and smell the coffee but I thought I could share the reasons why my performance was not top notch as he had expected. That was the mistake, opening up about my private life to my boss.

Looking back on how he used this information to manipulate me it's a wonder I did not just quit immediately or sense that he was using that information against me. Not that sharing is bad but there are matters that are best kept away from work. I believed for a while that the reason for my dissatisfaction at work was my personal problems only to take time out and do an exercise called clearing out did I realize my frustrations were coming from the work I did and not my personal life.

It sank in and I thought I could easily solve this by confronting my boss about this and I made it worse. The next thing I knew, rules and regulations which were more controls around me were put in place and I was suffocating. Had I not tried to be diplomatic and followed all rules by the book to better my situation at work so I could perform better?

The more days passed by, the more I was convinced that the situation was not improving and in any case I was losing out more as my spirit, I realized, was broken. The tough decision of quitting had to be done only because I felt I was not gaining what I had set out to do and skills to gain and the self development that was the overall mission.

I should have listened to my instincts and not shared my personal dilemma to my boss. Drawing the line between work and life is a lesson I have taken home and working on how much I can share at work and how I can balance my life and work.

DON'T SLEEP IN THE BUS, EPISODE #3
ID: 201

I never learn! After falling asleep in the bus twice, I did it yet again, this time abroad.

Taxis in Singapore are kind of expensive, so when I was assigned to work at one of the industrial parks, yet I had to "live" in the city because that is where the headquarters are – I had to take the bus. It was a 30-minute one way travel time every day; this time included the transfer between buses, the waiting time, and everything in between.

Mistakes In Life: The Path To Wisdom

It became a routine for me for around a week, until one morning after the previous night's drinking session. This time I remember probably the first 10-minutes of the bus stopping at different pickup points, as well as the person who sat beside me.

Because I-didn't-know-how-many-minutes had passed, I woke up in a strange place, where there were buses all over. I was sweating when I woke up because there was no air-conditioning on the bus, and I was seated in the upper deck of the bus. There goes the oh-man-I-fell-asleep-again syndrome.

Adrenalin rushed through me as soon as I saw that I had 12 missed calls – from my boss! Oh my, it was my last day at the customer's site, and I was due to present the results of my case study. I felt shivers down my spine, and I was already shaking in panic. I rushed down and found the driver of the bus – asleep too. Poor auntie driver was too tired, she didn't even notice me get off the bus. As I walked towards what I assumed to be the exit, the other drivers/employees were looking at me. I didn't care, all I had in my mind was what to tell my boss. I actually didn't turn up for work that time, I was almost AWOL but I made an alibi that I was terribly sick, with possibly the flu. I learned that the customer was disappointed by this, but was still also concerned that I got sick.

All this chaos – because of falling asleep on the bus.

From this moment on, I declined "drinking sessions" during the weekdays, especially if there were big events coming up at work. I have been OK so far (with the not-sleeping part), but I still go out for weekday fun at times. This time, being more conscious about work events that need to be anticipated for.

HIGH-HEELED DISASTER

ID: 251

As a fashion enthusiast I have always loved wearing shoes that usually have 5 inches heels. Every time I saw a pair that I liked on a fashion magazine,

TV, or the internet, I'd go buy them right away. For a long time, I hadn't notice any pain in my feet or ankles. Until one night I was attending an office party to meet our new clients, which had required everyone to stand up and walk around the room for hours. All of a sudden I felt an intense throbbing in the arches of my feet and the cramps went slowly up my legs. The stabbing pain became more uncomfortable and so I excused myself and hurriedly went to the washroom. On my way, I had a panic attack so I fumbled. One of my colleagues caught me and asked if I was ok. I told her I needed to take my shoes off. She helped me with my shoes and I felt relieved when I took them off. I think my feet went black-and-blue with blisters all over them for being inside the shoes the entire time. The strain also made it nearly impossible for me to walk for a while; I saw myself wearing flats on the days following the incident. I have avoided wearing very high heels regularly and tried to switch from flats to rubber from time to time after then.

PROCRASTINATE NOT – THINGS WILL SURELY CATCH UP

ID: 446

I used to work with a non-profit organization where medical and dental insurance was free. At some point during fieldwork, I contracted some form of typhoid fever that was believed to have been wiped out many years ago. I spent four days in the hospital and since my organization has a walk-in policy in which the accredited hospital can provide us with certain privileges, I took the VIP room wherein I did not have to share with anyone, plus getting all the perks of being in such hospital room. I got discharged eventually after being put on an IV drip for a while. Months later, the insurance provider sent me an email to follow a link and indicate to them the kind of illness I had contracted in which the hospital charged my organization a few thousand dollars. At the time I was reading my email, I was distracted by other activities and decided to put it off until another time. A day went by and then another until it had completely slipped my mind. The next thing I knew I received a notice that they were going to kick me out of the insurance service because I had not replied immediately to their previous inquiry. Of course I could not whip up any forms of excuse other than I procrastinated. Indeed, I was removed from their list of insurance beneficiaries and in case I would get sick again, I would not receive any more of the privileges. I regretted dismissing that email which was too important. I never got sick again though, thankfully enough, but I learned my lesson in the most embarrassing way because my manager predictably was notified about my inaction. Everyone else knew of the incident and they talked and talked about it for a while. But I could only take responsibility for it. So whenever I receive an email especially a very important one, I respond to it as soon as I finish reading it or within the same day if I have the resources which the sender requires of me so I don't have to go through the same embarrassment from procrastination.

EXCEPTIONAL ANGER

ID: 593

Thirteen years ago, there was a cat living in my house. It was brown with beautiful eyes and my mother really loved the cat. Naturally, I dislike cats and kicked it whenever it did something that I didn't like. One day, my mom and dad were planning to go a long way to visit relatives and they told me to keep my eyes open and clean the house. I accepted their command and started to do what they told me. I had been continuously working for six hours and I finished at midday. Suddenly I heard something falling down in my bedroom. When I opened the door of my room, the new flat screen TV had fallen down and the screen was out of use. Beside the TV, the cat ate my burger that I put on the table. My face become red and I couldn't explain how I felt at that moment. I dragged the cat and decided to throw the cat in the nearby river. Then I put the cat into an old luggage bag and threw it into the river. Then my face became normal. When I think about it now, I wish I didn't throw the cat in the river but I did it. The next day my mother searched for the cat but she couldn't find him and I didn't tell her. Now, I have changed my attitude toward cats. Now I love cats more than my mom.

My Lan T. Tran

CLOSING NOTES

Thank you for reading this book. I hope you enjoyed it and/or learned something valuable that you could apply to your own life or maybe help another person who is making the same or similar mistake to one of the stories you've read.

If you have stories of the mistakes you've made and the lessons you've learned from them and would like to share to help other people, please create an account on www.MistakesInLife.net and post your stories there or you may send it to support@mistakesinlife.net and it will be posted as Anonymous. Your stories might help someone save a lot of time, energy, money, and/or heartache.

If you would like to make a donation to help keep this project going, please go to www.MistakesInLife.net and click on the Donation page. Thanks in advance!

May life treat you kindly and fill your days with happy surprises! ☺

With love,
My Lan T. Tran

Made in the USA
Charleston, SC
16 April 2014